MINIMALISM

A Bridge between
Classical Philosophy
and the
Bahá'í Revelation

William S. Hatcher

JUXTA PUBLISHING LTD. (HONG KONG)

Dedicated to John Compton and Philip Hallie,
who first opened up for me the world of philosophy,
and to W. V. Quine, whose clarity of mind has
showed all of us the way through the labyrinth.

ABOUT THE AUTHOR

William S. Hatcher is a mathematician, philosopher, and educator. He holds a doctorate in mathematics from the University of Neuchâtel, Switzerland, and bachelor's and master's degrees from Vanderbilt University in Nashville, Tennessee. A specialist in the philosophical interpenetration of science and religion, he has, for over forty years, held university positions in North America, Europe, and Russia,

Professor Hatcher is the author of over fifty monographs, books, and articles in the mathematical sciences, logic, and philosophy. He is one of eight Platonist philosophers listed for the second half of the twentieth century in the highly regarded Encylopédie Philosophique Universelle (Presses Universitaires de France, 1992).

ABOUT THE COVER

This sketch of an eye is based on a sketch in the notes of René Descartes. The eye, as the conduit through which we view and understand our environment, serves as a metaphor for the nature of human perception and our understanding of the universe and our own existence.

This title is part of the Books for the World series. The Books for the
World series aims to bring diverse literature to people around the
world by directing all proceeds from sale of a title into donating the
same title to people who otherwise could not afford it as well as
offering library donation programs and free electronic books which can
be used for local printing and distribution.

www.juxta.com

The Web site for this book can be found at:

minimalism.hatcher.org
or
minimalism.juxta.com

Cover Design by David Dayco (www.epiphanygraphics.ca)

CONTENTS

INTRODUCTION

There can be no serious doubt that the modern period, both in philosophy and in science, begins with René Descartes (1596-1650). Modern science is squarely based on Descartes' fusion of Greek geometry and Arabic algebra into a single unified discipline, algebraic geometry. Greek geometry arose out of a logical analysis of our global intuition of spatial objects (e.g., a circle is perfectly and uniformly round). Algebra was the study of the formal rules for operating with pure quantities (numbers), whether considered as instruments for measuring (e.g., lengths of line segments) or for counting (assigning cardinalities to collections of discrete objects). Algebraic geometry allowed for both the quantization of spatial intuition and for the transfer of geometric intuition to algebra. Within one generation, Newton and Leibniz had invented calculus and Newton had written *Principia*—arguably the greatest single book of science ever written—which established the law of gravitation and showed how all the then-known science could be deduced from a few basic principles.

Descartes' philosophy was really a modern form of Platonism, in which innate ideas, implanted in the human mind by God, played a similar role to the universal forms of Plato's philosophy. The important shift, however, was that Descartes' approach was bottom-up instead of top-down. It began with undisputable facts of the human condition (we are conscious, self-aware beings with no intrinsic measure of absolute truth), and moved upward towards the absolute (whose existence we can deduce from the nature of our innate ideas). For Plato, empirical observation and logical analysis were only exercises—vulgar approximations of the true knowledge that came only with the clear intuition of the forms. For Descartes, however, logical analysis and empirical observation were an integral part of true knowledge itself. For him, knowing meant knowledge of causal relationships between phenomena, the latter giving rise to laws which could be expressed in the exact language of mathematics. For Plato, mathematics was important, but primarily as an analogy of the process of perceiving the forms—and of course a prime example of the usefulness and applicability of such knowledge.

Following Galileo's dictum that "nature is writ in the language of mathematics," Descartes conceived of a breathtaking programme: to build a complete description of the whole of reality in exact, mathematical language. The immense success of Newton's *Principia,* following so closely on the heels of Descartes' articulation of his method, provided highly convincing evidence that such a programme was realizable and indeed that its achievement was close at hand. The classic, Platonic paradigm of design was replaced by the Cartesian-Newtonian paradigm of creation through the establishment of lawful, cause and effect relationships.

Of course, there is no fundamental contradiction between the two approaches. The Platonic design paradigm focuses on the abstract structures underlying material reality, while the Cartesian-Newtonian paradigm focuses on the causal processes by which material reality has come to reflect these structures. Perhaps Plato would have argued that, once we really understand the structures themselves (by perceiving clearly their form), there is nothing else worth knowing about reality. But such a viewpoint neglects the immense power that comes from the practical knowledge of how to produce and reproduce these causal processes and therefore to use the resulting configurations for our own purposes (i.e., to satisfy our own subjective desires and accomplish subjective goals). In other words, pure Platonism is somewhat passive in its epistemological stance: we learn the truth in order to conform ourselves to it—to avoid making mistakes in our interactions with the world. In the Cartesian-Newtonian paradigm, we use our knowledge of causal relationships not only to understand reality but also to change it or, more precisely, to change our relationship to it. To succeed, the human enterprise needs knowledge that is both true (accurate) and useful (for the satisfaction of human needs). The Platonic paradigm gives us truth without necessarily giving us utility. Pure empiricism—trial and error—gives us utility without formal or structural truth. The Cartesian-Newtonian paradigm seeks both truth and utility, transcendence and immanence.

However, it is now generally held that the Cartesian programme has failed. Descartes, it is now felt, asked for too much. By creating his spirit/matter, soul/body dualism, he has tried both to have his cake and eat it. For Descartes tacitly assumed that the effective causes of material phenomena were material and potentially observable, and his successor, Leibniz, made this assumption an explicit axiom of rationalism. If this is true, then we can practically explain everything in terms of process and simply forget about the Platonic realm of absolute, transcendent and spiritual truth. Knowledge of spiritual reality is deprived of any utility. It becomes, at best, a bourgeois luxury and, at worst, an obscuring encumbrance. Thus, the idea arose in the 19th and 20th centuries that materialism was adequate for science, if not for metaphysics, and that the whole concept of a spiritual (transmaterial) reality could be dispensed with.

However, modern developments in the hardest of sciences—logic, mathematics and physics—have shown unequivocally that materialism is not self-contained, that it is both philosophically and scientifically inadequate. The first such development was the undecidability principle of Heisenberg, that joint or simultaneous measurements of certain physical parameters are logically impossible. At first presented as only a practical or empirical limitation, the Heisenberg principle turned out to be a provable mathematical theorem within the Hilbert Space mathematical formulation of quantum mechanics. In this strong form, the Heisenberg principle can be stated as follows: no complete and exact description of physical reality is logically possible within the framework (and based on the axioms) of the Hilbert Space model of quantum mechanics.

As strong as the Heisenberg uncertainty principle may be, it does not in itself constitute a definitive refutation of Descartes' programme, because it leaves open the possibility that some other, more adequate formulation of quantum mechanics may remove Heisenberg indeterminacy and restore completeness to our mathematical descripiton of reality. However, this possibility was destroyed by the phenomenon of Gödel incompleteness (see IV.2). In 1931, Gödel showed, by an ingenious but straightforward argument, that any objectively specifiable mathematical system which is rich enough to contain the basic axioms and lexicon of arithmetic is incomplete, meaning that the system will contain true propositions that cannot be proved (nor their negations disproved).[1] In other words, there cannot exist any complete and exact description of reality. As John Myhill once put it: there is no nonpoetical description of the whole of reality.

The icing on Gödel's cake was provided more recently by Roger Penrose who applied Gödel's results to show that the human brain cannot be a deterministic device (machine).[2] We now know certainly that any substantial theory of reality represents a compromise (trade-off) between exactness and adequacy. In particular, totally exact theories (i.e., objectively specifiable formal theories) will, if non-trivial, always be incomplete (i.e, there will be propositions stateable in the language of the theory which can be neither proved nor disproved within the theory). Such theories will be exact descriptions of a circumscribed part of reality, but never of the whole.

The question naturally arises as to whether there exist theories which describe the totality of reality (thus, necessarily in metaphorical, extramathematical language). Such complete but inexact theories would be the polar complement of the exact partial theories of science. That such theories do exist is the basic premise of a certain conception of religion first fully articulated by Bahá'u'lláh (1817-1892), founder of the Bahá'í Faith. According to this view, the revelations of the great prophet-founders of the major religious systems of history, insofar as the contents of these revelations have been accurately recorded and pre-served, each constitute complete, though highly metaphorical and nonlinear, descriptions of reality. In particular, Bahá'u'lláh makes the claim of completeness for his own revelation, contained in over one hundred volumes of writings composed during the period 1852-1892.

According to the Bahá'í teachings, God has ordained two sources of valid knowledge of reality: science and revelation. The object of knowl-edge is the same in both cases, but the methods are different. Science operates by systematizing the otherwise spontaneous experience of con-crete reality and, by inductive generalization coupled with creative conceptualization, moving upward towards abstract, general principles (laws), which are then tested through further experience by the system-atic application of certain *verification procedures* (see II.4). The language of science is deliberately *linear*—eschewing metaphor and multiple meaning—and *minimalist*—accepting the objective existence of only those nonobservables strictly necessary to an explanation of observable configurations (which, as it turns out, is still quite a bit). Thus, the strengths of science are clarity, precision, and applicability (practical-ity). Its limitations derive primarily from its partialness (specialization, fragmentation), relative incompleteness, and general lack of a global vision.

Revelation is based on the divine authority of the Prophet or Mani-festation of God, and is the perfect complement to science. In contrast to the language of science, the language of revelation is *nonlinear* (ex-tensive use of metaphor and multiple meaning) and *maximalist* (as rich as possible, freely referring to nonobservables). Moreover, Bahá'u'lláh repeatedly affirms that His revelation is a complete (though nonlinear and inexhaustible) description of reality.

In contrast to the language of science, the language of revelation tends to be *top-down*—beginning with certain very general and universal principles and then moving by specification and individuation towards the application of these principles to concrete human experience. Thus, the strengths of revelation are its adequacy and its completeness, but its limitations (from the human point of view) lie in its complexity and the consequent frequent lack of an obvious linear meaning for a given portion of the revelatory text. The student of revelation must be prepared to struggle to understand the different levels of meaning enfolded in the revelation.

To sum up: the study of science consists in confronting our experience of the phenomena of reality, formulating certain propositions whose meaning is *a priori* clear (because of the linearity of scientific language), and applying appropriate verification procedures to determine the truth or falsity of these propositions. We call this whole process *verification* for short. Studying the revelation consists in confronting various portions of the text of revelation, focusing on certain statements whose truth is known *a priori,* and then striving to determine various linear meanings of these statements. We will give the name *explication* to this process (meaning to *make explicit* the meanings of the text). Thus, for science, clarity of meaning is given *a priori* but truth is determined *a posteriori.* For (revealed) religion, truth is given *a priori,* but meaning is determined *a posteriori.*

The persistent, conjoint application of scientific verification on one hand, and of careful explication of revelation on the other, yields the very thing we need for the successful prosecution of the human enterprise: truth—accurate, useful, and adequate knowledge of reality. We may reasonably conclude, therefore, that the method of Bahá'í scholarship is the systematic, judicious, and disciplined application, to the data of reality, of the twin processes of scientific verification and textual explication (most particularly applied to the texts of the Bahá'í revelation).

The Bahá'í theory of revelation rests totally on the infallibility of the Manifestation, and it would be tempting to suppose that, if this theory is correct, there would be no need for the enterprise of philosophy (other than, perhaps, the philosophy of science on one hand, and the theology and philosophy of religion on the other). The thesis of the present monograph is that such is not the case. Philosophy and philosophical discourse are still needed as a crucial link between the minimalistic exactness of science and the maximalistic completeness of revelation. Without this philosophical bridge, we cannot effectively apply the insights of revelation in a practical way nor can we effectively use science to gain an overall perspective on reality.

Thus, though the present author accepts the validity of the Bahá'í theory of revelation, our monograph cites only a few passages from the Bahá'í writings. Moreover, even these quotations do not constitute appeals to authority but are given only to reinforce logical points that have already been made on other grounds.

As is explained in the course of the present monograph (I.1-3), the contribution of philosophy to the human enterprise derives from the mind's ability to make its current activity into its future object of inquiry. This process of *reflection* leads to a heightened sense of self-awareness because it enables us, however imperfectly and relatively, to gain objective self-knowledge through progressive self-objectification.

Once the necessity of philosophy is acknowledged, two extreme positions are possible. The first is an objectivist (positivistic) reductionism which holds that there is nothing beyond that which can be objectified. This position holds that all knowledge, or at least all significant knowledge, can be obtained from the process of objectification. This view of philosophy is typical of skeptics, positivists, and scientific materialists generally. The second extreme position is that only the trivial can be objectified. The characteristic of significant knowledge is precisely its essential subjectivity—that it resists objectification. Postmodernism/deconstructionism, existentialism, and some forms of mysticism take basically this position.

Philosophy in the twentieth century has largely consisted of a rather unproductive pseudo-dialogue between these two positions, in which the strategy on each side has been to attack the most blatant weak points of the other. This has led each side to take some exaggerated stances that are self-defeating. On one hand, the subjectivists have come to view science, and its social offspring technology, as the root of all evil and the source of all human problems. Some have gone so far as to assert that the truth claims of science are no more valid than the truth claims of sorcery or primitive mythmaking. On the other hand, the reductionist/ materialist view has gone so far as to claim that basic human emotions such as love and loyalty are no more than primitive, irrational trash to be gradually discarded by the truly enlightened (see IV.1). Some philosophers have even suggested that sufficiently advanced electronic computers will constitute (or may already constitute) functional entities that are superior to human beings, in part because they lack the bothersome and irrational emotionality of humans.

These extreme positions are rather easy to refute (see IV.1-2). What is not so easy is to find a reasonable alternative to both of these extremes, an alternative that incorporates the obvious strong points of each. This is what the method we have here called *minimalism* seeks to do. But minimalism goes far beyond the attempt merely to seek a passive, *ad hoc* compromise between these extremes. Rather, minimalism is a proactive philosophy of truth-seeking which sees philosophy as a cooperative dialogue with reality rather than a polemical dialogue between proponents of various dogmatic points of view.

Some of the fundamental premises of minimalism are: (1) a significant (non-trivial) portion of human knowledge can be objectified (objectification is possible); (2) the whole of human knowledge cannot be objectified (total objectification is impossible); (3) everything which can be objectified should be objectified (objectification has a positive value); (4) the boundary between the objectifiable and the non-objectifiable cannot itself be objectified (we prove objectification only by accomplishing objectification); (5) valid human knowledge which resists objectification is not irrational but transrational (i.e., compatible with what has been correctly, non-reductionistically objectified); (6) objectification is primarily a means of obtaining clarity, rather than an end in itself.

Because minimalism renounces all claim to completeness (see (2) above), it can afford to be more strict and cautious with what it does objectify. In particular, minimalistic metaphysical concepts are all *empirically grounded* in that they represent straightforward generalizations from observable facts and configurations (see section V).

A particular feature of minimalism is its rigorous treatment of value notions and concepts. Indeed, if applied only to facts and theories, minimalism differs little from Descartes' original method, except (and this is crucial) for abandoning the Cartesian/Leibnizian principle that causes of material phenomena are necessarily material (see V.4 and note 53). As it turns out, regarding causality as a logical rather than a material or temporal relationship enables us to apply causal reasoning to certain metaphysical and value concepts in a coherent way.

Indeed, the one point of agreement between the two extremes of reductionism and subjectivism is that value notions cannot be treated objectively and rationally. For the reductionist, objectivity implies viewpoint neutrality which, in turn, implies value neutrality (the suspension of value judgements). Thus, in this view, objectification excludes values by its very nature. For subjectivists, the realm of values is too rich, varied, and fundamentally irrational to admit of rational treatment.

The minimalistic approach to dealing with values begins with the crucial observation that objectivity and objectification mean viewpoint explicitness, not viewpoint neutrality (see III.3). Once this point is clarified, it is seen that one can make value assumptions as clearly explicit as any other assumptions and thus achieve the same level of objectivity for values as for theories or facts.

Central to minimalism is the use of and reliance upon the modern logic of relations (see III.5-7). Indeed, in a certain sense, minimalism is just the application of relational logic to classical problems in philosophy that have, heretofore, been treated only with the classical attributional logic of Aristotle (if at all). Relational logic leads us to ask different kinds of questions than does a purely attributional logic. It turns out that certain difficult questions have much clearer answers from a relational viewpoint than from an attributional viewpoint.

A prime example of this logical shift is our treatment of the existence and nature of God (see V.7-8). Classical, attributional approaches have tried, without much success, to define God intrinsically as that Being whose nature has some attribute of necessity (e.g., necessary existence, necessary perfection). The difficulty with this approach has been to give any clear and coherent notion of the exact nature of the necessity involved. Moreover, the uniqueness attributed to God practically guarantees that no metaphysical attribute of God can be empirically grounded (i.e., because God is, by His very nature, different from every possibly observable configuration). Our approach is to define God relationally as a universal cause. This definition is not only empirically grounded, but gives us practical information about how God relates to reality. Of course, it does not solve the classical problem of defining God's intrinsic nature, but it shows rather that we do not have to solve this problem in order to discourse meaningfully about God and our relationship to Him.

Readers with no technical background whatever in logic or philosophy will probably experience some initial difficulty in following all the details of our exposition in III.5-6. In order to understand the subsequent exposition, it would be sufficient for the reader to assume the following points as having been demonstrated: (1) the notion of logical truth (universally valid truth) can be totally objectified; (2) similarly, the notion of logical implication or logical consequence can be totally objectified; (3) there does not exist, however, any mechanical means (computer algorithm) for determining, in all cases, whether a given proposition is logically true or whether a given proposition is a logical consequence of another proposition (logical truth and logical implication are thus not *calculable*); (4) logic therefore has the power of deriving the unobvious from the obvious through a finite sequece of individually obvious steps.

In all cases the logic referred to here is modern relational (non-modal) logic. This logic has already been the basis of the modern revolution in mathematics and physics. Moreover, it is the ultimate basis both of computer architecture (hardware) and computer programming (software). Indeed, it was the remarkable success of formalization and objectification based on relational logic that gave impetus to the extreme of reductionism. Had we not had such unanticipated and unprecedented success in objectifying large areas of human knowledge, through the application of relational logic, it is highly unlikely that the philosophy of materialistic reductionism would ever have gained so many adherents.

For example, success in artificial intelligence (such as chess playing programs) have led many to conclude that all human mental functions might eventually be totally objectified, thus eliminating human subjectivity as a necessary adjunct to human thought. It is only with the advent of Penrose indeterminism (i.e., the human brain is not wholly deterministic) that confidence in this ultimte reductionism has begun to fade.

Our application of relational logic to problems in classical philosophy can thus be seen as the extension to philosphy of those modern methods which have already proven themselves in science. Thus, although our proof of the existence of God as universal cause (section V) is certainly interesting in itself, we present it primarily as a detailed application of the method of minimalism to a classical problem in philosophy. Other examples exist and could be given.

Thus, by what it actually accomplishes, minimalism destroys the widely-held idea that rigorous formal methods are restricted to and appropriate only for materialist science and that religion and metaphysics must proceed by other methods, if they are to have any justification at all. By successfully applying relational logic to metaphysical and ethical questions, we have made significant steps towards showing that reality is a unified whole, and that a considerable portion of human knowledge about metaphysical and ethical reality can be objectified. In other words, we are no longer justified in equating materialism with reason and logic and religion/metaphysics with subjective intuition alone.

Looked at another way, minimalism shows that there are general logical principles which are common to all intellectual endeavors, regardless of the domain of investigation in question. At the same time, minimalism's recognition of the limits of objectification shows that transrational intuition is an essential part not only of religion but of all intellectual enterprises including science. This is the sense, then, in which minimalism constructs a viable alternative to the extreme positions of reductionism, on one hand, and subjectivism, on the other. As we have seen, this alternative is not just a compromise position or a passive middle ground, but a proactive philosophy which yields genuine results.

I. THE NATURE OF THE PHILOSOPHICAL ENTERPRISE

I. PHILOSOPHY AS THE PURSUIT OF TRUTH

There is a broad range of opinions concerning the nature of philosophy. Some may regard it as no more than a sophisticated word game played by intellectuals, while others see it as a vital enterprise in which we engage ourselves wholly in a search for the meaning and truth of our existence. Still others see philosophy as a useful vehicle for intellectual debate and clarification of opinions, but not necessarily for the attainment of truth. Philosophy is the counterpart, in the sphere of intellectual activity, of artistic enterprises, such as music or painting, in which all can participate usefully but only a few do exceptionally well.

The more general an activity, the more difficult to define it precisely. George Bernard Shaw illustrated this principle by defining music as "the least obnoxious form of noise"—a logically impeccable definition that tells you nothing whatsoever about music. Attempts to define philosophy can lead to similarly vacuous descriptions, and one can begin to wonder how intelligent and earnest people can dedicate their lives to an enterprise that they cannot even describe in precise terms.

What is minimally clear is that philosophy is an enterprise which pursues knowledge of reality. Such a pursuit involves at least three things: the pursuer (in this case human beings), the thing pursued, and the method of pursuit. The distinguishing feature of philosophical inquiry is its openness and universality: it has neither a privileged subject matter nor a privileged method. Philosophy is therefore different from religion, which does have a privileged subject matter, and from science, which has a distinctive method.

'Abdu'l-Bahá says that "Philosophy consists in comprehending the reality of things as they exist, according to the capacity and the power of man."[3] Here again, philosophy is different from science, which is quite happy to study things as they appear, and from religion, which invokes revelation and divine assistance, thereby going beyond the capacities and powers of natural man.

2. PHILOSOPHY AS REFLECTION

Philosophical knowledge is a kind of second-order knowledge born out of *reflection* (i.e., the capacity of the human mind to make its current activity into its future object of inquiry). Each time we execute such a reflexive act, we take one step upward in the infinite "ladder of abstraction." This process has a beginning—in the form of our immediate consciousness (awareness) of spontaneous sensory impressions and the subjective inner states they provoke—but no end, since nothing can prevent the reflexive inner move to a higher level of abstraction. We can thus think of the data of philosophy as reflections on reflections on reflections on ... [down to] the data of our immediate, unanalyzed and spontaneous experience of reality. Of course, at any stage of this process, we are free to choose just what part of our experience we reflect upon and just how we go about reflecting upon it. Hence, philosophy has both content and method, just no *privileged* content or method.

3. A BRIDGE BETWEEN SCIENCE AND RELIGION

Thus conceived, philosophy is a bridge between the minimalism of science, which tends, whenever a choice appears necessary, to prefer local exactness over global adequacy, and the maximalism of religion, which, if necessary, may sacrifice a certain degree of local precision to obtain what it judges to be a more globally adequate view of reality. At its most general level, philosophy includes all of science but only part of religion, since the irreducibly mystical dimension of religion seeks experience of and communion with the Divine and not just human knowledge about the Divine. Thus, doing philosophy carefully and well is an effective means of understanding the relationship between and interpenetration of science and religion. Even more pointedly: doing philosophy badly results in a faulty understanding of the relationship between science and religion.

Let us take a look at a few examples of philosophical issues which are crucial to a proper understanding of the relationship between science and religion.

II. THE INDIVIDUAL PRACTICE OF PHILOSOPHY

1. OBSERVATIONS AND ASSUMPTIONS

Our experience of reality is always partial and limited. Our perceptions are nothing more than a series of clichés which we mentally complete into a seamless whole. If you are standing close in front of the windowless outside wall of a house, you don't see the rest of the house. How do you know it is there if you can't see it? Of course, you know it was there when you saw it five minutes ago, but how do you know it is there now?

Indeed, since we only experience the present moment in any case, does the world we observed five minutes ago still exist? Or has it been destroyed and replaced by the present world, which in turn will disappear, to be replaced by the future world? If you say that of course the world of five minutes ago didn't disappear, then it must still exist. Where is it? Does it exist in another world parallel to this one? Maybe the universe bifurcates at every instant of time.

The answer to these questions is that we assume macrophysical objects to have relative stability, at least in the short term, and the world at the present moment to be a continuation of the world of five minutes ago. Moreover, these simplifying assumptions are both reasonable and functional; indeed we could hardly live without them. But the point is that they *are assumptions.* They come from us, not from our direct experience of the world itself. To say even that objects exist is an assumption which serves to simplify our view of the world by allowing us to conceive of a multitude of different sensations (colors, sounds, shapes, textures, noises, smells) as being produced by a single whole entity.

Thus, all of our knowledge, even of the simplest and most concrete thing, is a product of both the thing (the object) and our minds (the subject) which smoothly completes our partial and limited experience of the world through a multitude of (mostly unconscious) simplifying assumptions. This is the inescapable human condition. Our knowledge is always partly subjective (i.e., accompanied by mental constructs) no matter how exhaustive and precise may be the observations on which that knowledge is based.

The above is a small example of philosophy at work. These observations about the human condition belong neither to science nor to religion. Rather, they are made at a level of generality and abstraction that encompasses both science and religion. Every human being is subject to these conditions whether he likes it or not, and he cannot escape them through some act of faith, by wishing them away or by ignoring their existence.

2. INNER MODEL, POINT OF VIEW, REASON

Although these limitations are themselves inescapable, we nevertheless do have a certain degree of choice in the attitude we take towards them. There are roughly three logically possible approaches. Let us call them common sense, insanity, and reason. The common sense approach is the one taken by the vast majority of people. It consists in remaining largely unconscious of our simplifying assumptions, adjusting them on an *ad hoc* basis only when the circumstances of our lives force us to do so.

If, for example, our initial relationships in life have been based on genuine trust and loyalty, we may tend to assume that virtually everyone is trustworthy until we are victimized seriously by a duplicitous person. This experience will force us to face our assumptions and modify them to some extent.

One can also imagine the other extreme in which betrayal has pervaded our early relationships. We may then assume rather that people generally are untrustworthy and consequently find great difficulty in establishing trustful relationships in adulthood.

In other words, each of us has a unique personal history which we bring to every new encounter with reality. The sum of this history—the body of previous experiences and our assumptions about these experiences—constitutes our *inner model* of reality and determines thereby our *point of view* on the world. This inner model creates within us certain expectations about how reality *should* behave. These normative expectations will influence even our simplest perceptions of the world, sometimes leading us to suppress or omit evident aspects of the observed configuration and sometimes leading us to project or add wished-for elements that are in reality not present.

The common sense approach to life is essentially passive in that it allows the process of perception/assumption to go on rather spontaneously: we take our point of view as *normal* and *natural* until some experience of reality overwhelms us and forces us to revise our inner model, perhaps in spite of ourselves. Such experiences occur when our expectations about how reality should behave are not met. In the common sense approach to life, our subjective assumptions about reality may not be optimal, but they tend to be *functional* (i.e., we tend to make those assumptions which increase our ability to function in the world), at least in the short term. Part of our ability to function is our relationship with other human beings, and so the nature of our assumptions will be influenced by the assumptions of others. Our social environment serves as a reference group to which we turn for confirmation of our point of view. If we discover that certain of our assumptions are not in conformity with prevailing social norms, we will tend to readjust them in the direction of (our perception of) social norms. In this way, our inner model is not just an individual construct but also a social construct. It is a construct which is a compromise between the hard data from reality, on one hand, and certain individual and social needs, on the other.

The insane approach to life is based on the conviction that we can make gratuitous and arbitrary assumptions with impunity. In this case, we give priority to our needs over the data from reality in an egocentric attempt to make reality conform to our inner model rather than striving to have an inner model which conforms to reality. Hence, insane assumptions may often be dysfunctional: they actually decrease our ability to relate successfully to the world, to ourselves, and to others. If the inner needs which drive insane assumptions are strong enough, then we may not give them up even in the face of extreme contrary evidence. In this case, we may temporarily lose all autonomy of life processes and require therapeutic intervention to defeat the unhealthy pattern.

With the common sense approach we are at least aware that points of view other than our own are possible and perhaps legitimate, even though we take our own point of view as the most natural or normal. In insanity, we not only take our point of view as natural but in fact as the only possible point of view.

The third approach, which we have called reason, is an ongoing and deliberate attempt to become as aware as possible of our underlying assumptions. The ideal or goal of reason is to make our assumptions totally explicit. Reason is thus a proactive attempt to meet life *head-on* rather than passively as in the common-sense approach. Reason explicitly acknowledges the relativity of one's point of view. Indeed, in making our own assumptions explicit, we become aware of other possible assumptions and the rationale for them.

Moreover, making our assumptions explicit gives us greater autonomy and control over life processes. For once we have clearly identified our operational assumptions, we can apply logic to them and thereby foresee (predict) their long term consequences. With this knowledge, we can proceed to modify our assumptions in the light of the longer term, rather than just the short term as in the case of common sense, thereby optimizing our autonomy and functionality. In a certain sense, then, reason is just self-conscious common sense. The journey from common sense to reason is a journey of increasing awareness, consciousness, and self-knowledge.

3. KNOWLEDGE AND REALITY, SUBJECTIVITY AND OBJECTIVITY

One of the most contentious issues in the history of philosophy has been the question of the extent to which it is possible for us to have objective knowledge of reality. By *objective knowledge*, we mean a knowledge that is invariant under changes of point of view. The question itself already involves several assumptions: (1) there does exist a mind-independent (objective) reality whose intrinsic features or qualities are independent of the mental states of the knower; (2) it is in principle possible to apprehend these objective qualities, if not wholly and perfectly, at least to a significant degree; (3) it is possible to formulate or articulate this understanding in a manner that allows us to communicate it to others and to validate the independency (or invariance) of this understanding under certain changes of point of view (which we will call *transformations*).

The first assumption amounts to the proposition that reality is not just a mental illusion or figment of our imagination. The logical negation of this assumption yields *absolute subjectivism* or *solipsism*—the proposition that nothing exists outside of our subjective mental states. Very few thinkers or philosophers have ever held such a degree of subjectivism, although many would affirm that the world is to some extent *illusory* (i.e., that it presents to our perceptions a semblance of permanence and stability that it does not, in fact, possess). However, we reject as grossly unreasonable the belief that all our perceptions of everyday reality—including interactions with other people and experiences of physical pain—are pure products of our individual imagination.[4]

The second assumption is slightly more nuanced. It does not affirm that we have a perfect, exact or complete knowledge of objective reality, only that we can have a relatively significant and useful knowledge of objective qualities. The antithesis to this assumption holds that, although objective reality may well exist, we can have no significant knowledge of it. Let us call this view *radical subjectivism.*

The argument for radical subjectivism hinges on a logical *non sequitur* and runs something as follows: (a) what *is* knowledge, in the last analysis, but certain ideas, perceptions, and intuitions; (b) ideas, perceptions and intuitions are all subjective, mental entities; (c) thus, all knowledge is subjective; (d) hence, there is no such thing as objective knowledge (i.e., knowledge of objective qualities and properties of reality).

The fault in the argument lies in the implicit identification of knowledge itself with the object of knowledge. We have already pointed out above that human knowledge consists of an inner model which we construct on the basis of our interactions with reality. This inner model is a configuration of internal, mental states and therefore wholly subjective in nature. However, the ontological status of ideas as mental entities says nothing whatsoever about whether a given idea is an accurate reflection of an objective entity.

An inner model relates to reality like a map relates to a territory. Ontologically, a map of Canada has nothing in common with Canada. Canada is a geographical territory made up of earth, water, forests, cities, people, and animals, while a map of Canada is a piece of paper on which various colors have been impressed. What makes this mass of colored fibers into a map *of* Canada is the existence of an appropriate correspondence between certain points on the map and certain real locations in Canada. Similarly what makes our inner model a model *of* reality is the existence of a correspondence between certain features of the subjective model, on one hand, and certain features of objective reality, on the other. Whether a given idea is true or only a vain idea depends on whether an appropriate relationship exists between the idea and some portion of objective reality. 'Abdu'l-Bahá has expressed this conception of the nature of knowledge in the following terms:

> *Reflect that man's power of thought consists of two kinds. One kind is true, when it agrees with a determined [reality]. Such conceptions find realization in the exterior world; such are accurate opinions, correct theories, scientific discoveries and inventions.*

> *The other kind of conceptions is made up of vain thoughts and useless ideas which yield neither fruit nor result, and which have no reality. No, they surge like the waves of the sea of imaginations, and they pass away like idle dreams.*[5]

Let us sum up briefly. A human idea is a subjective mental entity, by its very nature. Some ideas are *vain* in that they do not correspond to any reality outside of themselves. Other ideas are *true* in that they reflect or mirror some configuration in reality via an appropriate correspondence between these ideas and certain features of the configuration. The constellation of ideas that represents our current view of the world constitutes our inner model of reality and determines the point of view from which we perceive further input from reality. Reality is like a territory and our inner model is like a map we have made of that territory.

Pursuing the map/territory analogy a bit further, let us observe that there are fundamentally two ways that a map can be inaccurate: it can lack a proper correspondent to some feature that exists in reality or else it can contain elements which have no correspondent in reality. In the first instance, we say the map is *inadequate,* meaning that it under-represents reality. In the second instance we say the map is *false,* meaning that it portrays or represents reality as having features that in fact do not exist.

Since our inner model is always based on partial information, it is bound to be inadequate in various respects, and since it reflects not only our perceptions but also our desires and needs, it is bound to be false in certain respects. Our total inner model can thus be true and adequate in some respects and false or inadequate in others. Thus, when applied to our total inner model, the terms *true* and *false* are, in this precise sense, relative: we can speak of our inner model as being largely or mostly true or, on the contrary, largely or mostly false.

So, we have *knowledge of reality* to the degree that our inner model is adequate and true. To know something is to have an accurate inner model of it. This is the nature of knowledge. The knowledge (inner model) itself is a subjective entity, but the reality represented by the inner model (what the knowledge is *about*) may well be objective.

The radical subjectivist fallacy, then, turns on a confusion between the ontological status of ideas as mental entities, on one hand, and the ontological status of the object of knowledge, on the other. It confuses the map with the territory. Thus, whenever we speak of ideas as being objective or subjective, we must be careful to make precise whether we are talking about the ideas themselves or the reality reflected by those ideas.[6]

4. TRUTH VS. VERIFICATION

Our refutation of radical subjectivism justifies assumption (2): it is in principle possible to obtain knowledge of objective reality. However, assumption (2) does not guarantee that we will in practice be successful in obtaining knowledge of reality; it only says that it is *prima facie* reasonable to pursue such knowledge. The question of how, in practical terms, we actually go about this knowledge-seeking enterprise consti-tutes the branch of philosophy known as *epistemology.*[7]

Our inner model is, as we have seen, a mosaic of true and false elements. But we experience our inner model as a seamless whole. We have no direct insight into its false aspects, because, for us, our inner model *is* (our perception of) reality. It would be logically impossible for us knowingly to maintain a false element in our inner model, because as soon as we realized its falsity it would no longer be a part of the model! In other words, we could not truly perceive grass as red while *knowing* it is really green. To know grass is green is to perceive it as green (remem-ber the correspondence between the map and the territory).

Thus, it is important to distinguish between the *fact* of our inner model being false in some respect, and our awareness of that fact. To see this more clearly, think of your inner model as the set of all beliefs that you hold—all the propositions about the world that you currently accept as true. On the one hand, you are convinced that each of your beliefs is true, because the instant you doubt a given proposition, it ceases to be one of your beliefs. On the other hand, given what we know about the limitations of human knowledge, *some* of your current beliefs are bound to be false.[8] You just don't know which ones.

We are thus led to yet another distinction—the distinction between truth and verification. Truth refers to the accuracy of the correspondence between our inner model and some portion of reality. But our inner model can be inaccurate without our awareness of this fact. Verification refers to the process of evaluating the accuracy of our inner model.

The verification process involves a comparison between our inner model and the feedback we get from certain particular encounters with reality. These *verification encounters* seek to test some particular part of the inner model about whose validity we are concerned. Of course, every interaction with reality gives us some feedback about our inner model, but purely spontaneous encounters may not give us the precise information we need to validate the portion that concerns us at the moment. Therefore, verification encounters are usually not spontaneous but are rather deliberately structured and contrived by us for the very purpose of testing a particular part of our model.

More exactly, in verification encounters we seek deliberately to *falsify* some aspect of our model (i.e., to induce encounters with reality in which the feedback information clearly and consistently contradicts our model). The logic of falsification derives from the fundamental observation that a truly accurate inner model is the one thing that *cannot* be legitimately falsified.

On one hand, if we suspect our map to be inadequate in some respect, then we will attempt to induce the experience of a real event that has no counterpart in our current map. On the other hand, if we suspect that our map contains elements having no real correspondant, then we will strive to bring about those conditions which our model prescribes as sufficient to produce the event in question. If our model is false, then what the model says will happen, simply won't happen. This systematic exploitation of deliberately contrived experiences of reality is what is popularly known as *experimentation*.

To ascertain, through verification, that our model is inaccurate is only the first step in a process of identifying precisely the erroneous elements and then finding an appropriate correction. This can sometimes be a short, straightforward process, but is often long and difficult, involving many false starts and periods of anguishing uncertainty about just how much of our model may have to be discarded or modified.

Failure to distinguish between truth and verification leads to another, weaker version of subjectivism, which we will call the *positivist* fallacy. This fallacy runs something as follows: since (as we falsely suppose) truth is verification, then the only true ideas are those we have verified to be so. No matter how apparently true a given idea may seem, it cannot be held to be genuine knowledge until it has passed our verification procedures. However, these procedures involve knower-initiated interactions which modify the nature of reality. The knower is no longer just a passive observer but also a participant—a part of the very reality he seeks to know. The feedback information generated by verification procedures is actually *created by* the action of the knower. Thus, the only thing we actually know is the reality created by our own verification procedures.

We therefore conclude that it is practically impossible to gain knowedge of objective reality *as it is,* because we ourselves are always in the way. We can only know reality as we contrive it to be. In other words, radical subjectivism may be theoretically false but it is practically true because human limitations prevent any significant degree of practical verification of affirmations about objective reality as it is.[9]

Besides the falsity of the initial premise, this fallacy also trades on an unstated presumption that reality should be chaotic, with very few regularities. Historically, most successful scientific theories have been based on bold generalizations (assumptions) from fairly limited empirical evidence. The fact that such highly theoretical constructs have been successfully verified empirically suggests that reality is in fact highly ordered and highly structured, with deep and subtle regularities. In other words, we might have pursued empirical verification as rigorously and systematically as possible and never verified anything because there would have been nothing to verify!

Subjectivist skeptics have pointed out that we tend to presume regularities from very little experience. They think we project imagined regularities onto reality with little empirical justification. The young child presumes that his room and bed and mother will be there tomorrow as they are today, but he has not consciously verified this assumption. The fact that this stability is actually true does not impress those who identify truth with verification. According to a certain brand of skepticism, the child has no right to presume a stability that he has not consciously verified. Moreover, the poor little thing is even ignorant of the fact that he has no right to know what he knows.

The point is that if the world were in fact extremely chaotic, unlawful, and unpredictable, then our inner models would also be chaotic and unstable—a reflection of the real state of the world. We would frantically move from one assumption to another, only to encounter yet another empirical refutation. But the fact is that our experience verifies our assumptions of stability and order more often than not.

That this order or regularity is often inferred from experience and not directly observed is extremely strong evidence in favor of *Platonism* or *realism,* which holds that there is an objective and rational order underlying the phenomena of reality. In other words, *the success of modern science has given a strong empirical ground to Platonism.* For most of us, this is good news and validates Descartes' contention that "God is not a deceiver."

Nevertheless, skeptics of various stripes—positivists, postmodernists and deconstructionists—continue their assault on realism, mainly by pointing out just how subjective our theories are and how difficult the verification procedures may be, at least in certain cases. Moreover, these criticisms often involve both the radical subjectivist fallacy of identifying the inner model with reality and/or the positivist fallacy of identifying truth with verification, all seasoned with a strong unstated bias against philosophical realism.[10]

5. INTERFERENCES BETWEEN THE KNOWER AND REALITY

But how do we deal with the fact that the process of verification can indeed interfere with or modify reality? We do this by incorporating the knower-reality interaction into our model—by making it explicit. This is done by requiring that verification procedures be invariant under certain changes of viewpoint.

For example, in physics, this approach began when, following the results of the Michelson-Morley light experiment (1897), Einstein made the explicit assumption that the speed of light was the same for all observers. This led to the theory of relativity, which is based on the assumption that all physical observations remain unchanged under uniform rectilinear motion. In simple terms, this means that you and I will never have any way of verifying whether or not we are both at rest or moving uniformly together in a given direction.

Thus, rather than being the destruction of science, the realization that observer-reality interactions affect verification has simply led to a more adequate model of reality. After all, we humans are part of objective reality and so there is nothing strange or unnatural about having to take this into account in building our models.

Subjectivist critics of science might acknowledge this, but would insist this fact implies that the verification process is always relative and never absolute, because we can never exclude absolutely the possibility that our verifications are tainted with some undetected knower-reality interactions. This observation is correct, as has been demonstrated in twentieth century science by the appearance of a number of *indeterminacy principles* (Heisenberg in physics, Gödel in mathematics). However, the relativity of our verification procedures already follows from the fact that our models are always based on partial information. The indeterminacy principles are simply one example of how the finiteness of human knowledge can express itself.

The relativity of the verification process raises the possibility of an infinite regress in which we verify truth, evaluate our verification, check our evaluation, etc. Indeed, the move from truth to verification is a move up the ladder of abstraction. First we had a territory and a map. Then we made the map into the territory (the object of knowledge) and the verification procedure became the new (higher order) map. Thus, verification is also a form of knowledge, but of a second order. It is knowledge about knowledge—what in philosophy we call meta-knowledge. But there is no absolute end to this process. We can make verification into the territory and then we will have meta-meta-knowledge, and so on. Such is the flexibility and openness of philosophy.

Classical philosophy tended to consider that infinite regresses were logically contradictory and therefore unacceptable. When confronted with the possibility of such a regress, as we are with the hierarchy of knowledge, meta-knowledge, etc., classical philosophy would find a way out of the infinite regress by appealing to some absolute principle. For example, Aristotle declares that an infinite regress of causes is impossible and therefore concludes that there must be an absolute (first) cause.[11]

If we applied such a move in the present context, we would conclude that since the infinite regress of meta-meta- ... meta-knowledge is not possible, there must be some point of absolutely certain knowledge. However, from modern mathematics we know that infinite regresses are not contradictory and in fact occur frequently in nature. Thus, we must accept the plausibility of the relativity of knowledge represented by the infinite regress of truth, verification, evaluation of verification, etc.[12]

In the light of this more sophisticated understanding of infinity, fundamentally two positions are possible. One is taken by postmodernist critics of science, who say that once the relativity of scientific knowledge is admitted, then the truth claims of science and philosophy become no more valid than any other truth claims, such as those of occultists, sorcerers, or mythmakers. Everybody is doing the same thing: constructing an inner model of reality based on their perceptions and verifying their model according to their particular criteria. Beyond that, there is no way of judging which of two models is, in any sense, better or more accurate than the other.

This position might be called *total relativism,* meaning that once any degree of relativity or uncertainty has been admitted, then it follows that all points of view are epistemologically equivalent. The question is whether and to what degree such a leap from *any* relativity to *total* relativity is justified. It is easy to see, from both the logical and the historical perspective, that it is not.

The other position, then, is that the process of iterating or repeating verification procedures, starting with some body of empirical data, leads to a progressive refinement of the inner model, and a gradual sharpening of our point of view. The process of gradual refinement of our models is an example of *convergence,* another modern notion connected with infinite regresses. The simple point is that there may always be inaccuracies in our models, *but not always the same inaccuracies.* For example, as we resolve uncertainties on a given level, we may create new, more refined uncertainties on a higher (meta) level, but we have nonetheless progressed in our knowledge, because something that was previously unknown is now known, and nothing that was previously known is lost. We can therefore think of our successive models as an increasingly more accurate representation of reality, and this process can continue indefinitely.

Our analysis has shown that the pursuit of absolute certainty is an unrealistic philosophical ideal. However, the process of convergence means that the admitted relativity of our knowledge can imply relative certainty rather than relative ignorance. To say that our knowledge is relative means that there is always a logical possibility of error, but not always a reasonable plausibility of error. There is an immense difference between a simple *possibility* and a high degree of *probability*. This difference has often been ignored or discarded by subjectivist critics of science, and especially by those who are inclined to make the leap from any relativity to total relativity.

6. REFINING OUR MODELS: AN EXAMPLE FROM THE HISTORY OF SCIENCE

The process of the gradual refinement of our inner model might be thought of as an ongoing dialogue between ourselves and reality. Each encounter with reality gives us a certain feedback which either confirms what we already know, challenges what we already know, or simply gives us entirely new information. We then respond to this feedback from reality by adjusting our inner model in some appropriate way.

The history of science exhibits this progression extremely clearly. Consider, for example, the history of our model of the phenomenon of gravitation, from Aristotle to Einstein. Aristotle held that heavier objects fall faster than lighter objects. His reasoning was that the force of gravitation is directly proportional to the mass, and thus more massive objects would be subject to a stronger force of attraction and thus fall at a faster rate. For almost two thousand years, this remained the accepted model of gravity. Finally, Galileo's experiments showed that, neglecting air resistance, all objects fall at the same rate: the acceleration due to gravity is a constant. This fact refutes Aristotle's theory, but does not immediately give a correct theory to replace it.

It was Newton who found the correct theory: the force of gravity is directly proportional to the mass, as Aristotle had said, but is, at the same time, (quadratically) inversely proportional to the distance between the mutually attracting objects. Furthermore, the greater the mass of an object, the greater its *inertia* (i.e., its resistance to a change of state of motion). Simply put, it takes more force to move a big rock than it does to move a little one. Thus, as it turns out, the greater force of gravitational attraction of heavy objects is compensated by the greater inertia of the heavy object in such a way that the acceleration due to gravity is in fact constant (i.e., the same for all bodies). Moreover, Newton's model was verified empirically. In fact it correctly predicted the observed movements of the planets.

Newton actually defined force not as mass times acceleration, but rather as the rate of change of momentum (mass times velocity). Newton's successors assumed that mass was constant and only velocity varied. But, after 1905, when Einstein explicitly brought in the knower-reality interaction (the constancy of the speed of light), it was immediately deduced that, at extremely high velocities, mass actually increases. This permitted a simple mathematical correction (refinement) of the Newtonian model of gravity, an effect which was subsequently observed empirically when experimental technique allowed for the acceleration of small masses to velocities near the speed of light.

But Einstein's refinement did not contradict Newton's original theory in any way. In Einstein's model, force is still proportional to the rate of change of momentum. But now we know that both mass *and* velocity vary, and not just velocity as Newton's successors had presumed. Thus, from Aristotle to Einstein, there was a progressive refinement of our model of the phenomenon of gravitation in which, at each stage of the process, our map was modified to take into account a more accurate knowledge of the territory. Moreover, this is not the end of the story, because there is a fundamental incompatibility between our respective models of gravitation and of quantum mechanics, which is our model of the other three known basic forces of physics (the strong and weak nuclear forces and electromagnetism). So, a climb further up the ladder of abstraction is in store for us.

Our summary sketch here of the history of gravitation theory is, of course, vastly simplified. Progress in science is never a straightforward linear progression. Science grows by fits and starts, false directions and cul-de-sacs, serendipitous discoveries and sometimes incredibly outrageous theories. Nevertheless, that there has been and continues to be an overall progression and refinement in scientific knowledge is beyond any serious debate.

7. RELATIVITY AND SOCIAL SUBJECTIVISM

Although it may seem difficult for most of us to believe, there are otherwise intelligent people alive today who believe, in apparent sincerity, that the Newton-Einstein model of gravitation is a myth on an equal footing epistemologically with Hitler's theory of Aryan supremacy or Nietsche's strongly held belief in the intellectual inferiority of women. The ultimate roots of this antiscientist school of thought can probably be traced to Thomas Kuhn, and his work *The Structure of Scientific Revolutions,*[13] though his successors and interpreters have perhaps gone further than Kuhn himself in the direction of antiscientism.

Kuhn was essentially a socio-historian who focused his attention on science, however not on its content or epistemological method, but rather on the social behavior of scientists themselves in their pursuit of scientific knowledge. Kuhn observed that scientists were not the detached, objective observers they sometimes claimed to be, but were passionate human beings, full of prejudices and weaknesses. He showed how, at each stage of its development, the discourse of science reflected the emotional tenor of its times. Science is not somehow outside of society, but, like everything human, is a product of human culture.

On the basis of this undoubted truth, Kuhn's successors (and perhaps Kuhn himelf, though that is not wholly clear) concluded, essentially, that all cultural products have equivalent truth claims: since science is produced by culture, it is simply a reflection of culture and nothing more. Science is a "cultural myth" on a par with any other cultural myth.

As the reader may already see, this is just a social form of the radical subjectivist fallacy. The fact that our ideas are themselves subjective mental entities does not mean that these ideas are not true of an objective reality. In the same way, the fact that our scientific theories are socially constructed models does not mean that these models cannot be relatively accurate reflections of an objective reality. One has again uncritically transferred a property of the models themselves (in this case that they are cultural products) to the logical content of these models, a classical *non sequitur.*

It might seem that this social subjectivism would be easy to refute. Just point to the fact that Newton's theory of gravitation allows us, on the basis of a few simple calculations, to place a communications satellite in a fixed orbit with respect to the earth or to send men to the moon and get them back. This is certainly not true of many other cultural myths.

Those who attempt to dialogue with convinced postmodernists will discover that such an attempted refutation will likely not be met with any coherent direct answer. It will rather generate a stream of discourse justifying the fact that science is indeed a cultural product. True, but beside the point.[14]

Since postmodernism represents the ultimate attack on philosophical realism, it is useful, in closing this discussion, to make one further point. From a strictly logical point of view, it would be quite correct to say that we have no *a priori* guarantee that our infinite iteration of the verification process will converge (i.e. that it will lead to a progressive refinement of our model). Our experience of applying this method might well have been one of divergence and frustration. This is why the history of science is so important to this debate: because it shows that there has been a *de facto* convergence, whatever our anticipations may be or may have been. Thus, the success of such models as Newton's theory of gravitation constitutes strong empirical evidence in favor of philosophical realism: if there is no objective order in reality, then it becomes very difficult to account for such convergences as we have already experienced.

Or, put it another way. If, as we have already entertained above, the world were in fact totally chaotic, then indeed any cultural myth would be just as true as science, because all would be equally false. But in such a world, there would be no communications satellites or moon expeditions (or, alas, weapons of mass destruction).

III. COMMUNICATING PHILOSOPHICAL IDEAS

1. INTERSUBJECTIVE DIALOGUE

We have discussed assumptions (1) and (2) in the context of a correspondence or dialogue between our inner model and reality. Assumption (3) now raises the question of intersubjective dialogue, of communication between different knowers or subjectivities.

The parameters of intersubjective communication are determined by the intrinsic nature of subjectivity itself. We follow the tradition initiated by Descartes in considering consciousness or self-awareness as the primal and defining characteristic of the human being. The individual's consciousness creates an inner world of private states to which only that individual has direct access. Your consciousness consists precisely of *your* thoughts, feelings, and desires, and my consciousness consists of *my* thoughts, feelings, and desires. Neither has direct access to the inner states of the other. Indeed, if I had such access to your inner states and you to mine, we would be one consciousness and not two. Thus, the locus of our consciousness defines us. We *are* our consciousness—the sum total of all of those states to which only we have direct access.

Individual subjectivities are thus wholly non-intersecting. We can talk about and share our mutual subjectivities, but we cannot experience them. I have access to objective reality only through the inner sensations it induces within me, and I have access to your subjectivity only to the extent that you can communicate it to me in some manner, verbal or otherwise.

The primary means of intersubjective communication is language. For our minimalist purposes, it is sufficient that a given language consist, on the one hand, of signs or symbols and the relationships between them and, on the other hand, of significances or meanings that we attach to these signs or symbols. We say that language involves *syntax* (the relations between the signs) and *semantics* (the relationship between the signs and their meanings). By a *language* we thus mean a general, unified system of syntax/semantics. Each language is associated with a specific *linguistic community* of those people who share that language.

Our definition of a language is somewhat more restrictive than the usual linguistic characterization of natural language. However, our notion is surprisingly rich—much richer than might at first be supposed. Moreover, any reasonably developed natural language will contain at least the data we have sketched here.

The first and most basic point to make is that the syntax of a language is, by its very nature, more concrete than its semantics. Indeed, it is now known that, without significant loss in generality, we can assume that any language has a finite number of basic (or irreducible) signs, called *alphabetical letters,* and that all other syntactical expressions are finite linear sequences (strings) of these letters. Though signs are somewhat abstract (they are equivalence classes of *tokens* under the relationship *sameness of shape*), a token itself is a concrete entity that can be used to represent its equivalence class (sign) in all contexts.

Certain strings, having an appropriate syntactical structure, are designated as *meaningful expressions.* Any linear sequence of meaningful expressions is a *text* or a *discourse.*[15]

The meaning of an expression is itself partly syntactical (grammatical or formal) and partly semantic. The point is that a grammatically correct expression has an objective existence as a syntactical entity, independent of the meanings that may be attached to it. Determining that a text is grammatically correct, and thus meaningful, is purely objective, but determining what the meanings are, should be, or may be is highly subjective (see discussion below, pp. 48 ff.) This distinction between syntax and semantics is useful, because it allows us to agree straightforwardly on a certain number of basic issues, and thus to save our energy for a discussion of the more contentious and difficult semantic questions.

It is clear that meanings, whatever they may be, are not inherent in the objective syntactical entities (signs and expressions) themselves. Ontologically, meanings are ideas or, more precisely, a correspondence between syntactical entities and ideas. The process by which certain meanings become associated with a given text is a fairly complicated psycho-linguistic process that has been much studied. However, the essentials of this process are relatively clear and generally agreed upon: meanings derive from social interactions which develop, for the most part unconsciously, within a cultural community that has undergone a shared history. Specific cultures arise from specific histories, specific languages arise out of specific cultures, and specific texts occur within specific languages.

There are basically two ways for an individual to become part of a given linguistic community (i.e., to learn a language): immersion or translation. In the first instance, we immerse ourselves in the linguistic community and thereby assimilate spontaneously the conventions of its language. Immersion thus includes the process of growing up within a given linguistic community. Translation is the more self-conscious and deliberate process of learning a correspondence between the conventions of the previously unknown language and a language that is already known.

Although there are *nonverbal* forms of communication, many of these can also be represented by an appropriate language. In any case, for the time being we will restrict our attention only to those forms of communication which use some language. Thus, whenever we speak of intersubjective communication, we implicitly assume that a given language is involved. In sum, our *communication* with objective reality is mediated by the inner sensations induced by objective entities, and our communication with other subjects is mediated by a language.

From this perspective, intersubjective communication is a *sharing of meaning*. Communication begins when each of us confronts the same text (discourse), whether I am speaking to you, you to me, or some third party to both of us. The syntax is concrete and can be presumed to be perceived similarly by both of us. But to what extent do we understand the text in the same way?

The process by which a given subject attributes meaning to a text is called *interpreting (the text)*. A text is part of reality, and interpreting a text is part of the larger process of generating our inner model of reality. The extent to which our respective inner models or interpretations of a given text are similar is the extent to which, in a given instance, we have successfully communicated. We can again apply a map/territory analogy. The text is like the territory and the interpretation is like the map. We have communicated to the extent that we each make similar maps of the same territory.

Just as there is a difference between truth and verification, there is also a difference between communication and verifying that we have communicated. You and I may in fact have understood a given text in virtually the same way, but be unable to verify the similarity in our understandings. (Suppose, for example, that we have each read the same poem and interpreted it in virtually identical fashion, but that we do not even know each other.)

2. LIMITATIONS IN COMMUNICATION

In discussing our dialogue with objective reality, we realized that there are certain inherent limitations in our inner models deriving, on one hand, from the incompleteness of our information from reality and, on the other hand, from self-generated falsities arising from those needs and desires which we incorporate into our picture of reality. In the same way, our point of view will influence the way we interpret a given text. But, beyond that, we need to see that there are certain things that cannot ever, even in principle, be communicated from one subjectivity to another.

On the most basic level, it is clear that we will never be able to convey to another human being our own subjective experience. I can of course describe my experience, and you can acknowledge that my description seems to describe yours as well. Our experiences can be similar, but never identical, because my experience is just that—my experience— and thus not yours.

Consider, for example, that you and I are discoursing about our respective experiences of the beauty of the same red rose. Your experience of the rose will induce in you a complex of thoughts, feelings, and desires to which only you have access. Neither I nor any other can experience your feelings of the rose; we can each experience only our own feelings. Suppose that, in actual fact, I experience as *greenness* what you and others experience as *redness* and that, reciprocally, I experience as redness what you and others experience as greenness. There is no way we could ever discover and communicate this fact. I will simply have learned to associate the vocable *red* with what you and others experience as redness but which I experience as greenness. We will each classify the same objects as red or green and indeed will produce the same protocols under all circumstances. Yet, my perception of what we all call *red* will in fact be the same as your and others' perception of green.

Notice that it is possible to give a perfectly objective definition of, say, greenness as that quality of precisely those objects which absorb all the spectrum of white light except the green portion, which they reflect. The *green portion* of the light spectrum can likewise be defined objectively in terms of wave lengths as measured on a spectrograph.

Thus, in the same way that we have direct experience not of objects but of the subjective sensations induced by our encounters with objects, so in communication we do not have direct experience of another subjectivity but only of the descriptive protocol of the sensations experienced by the other. Strictly speaking, what we communicate to each other is not experience but our mutual understanding of experience.

Attempting to verify whether you and I have similar interpretations of a given text generates an infinite regress similar to the one generated when we attempt to verify the truth of an idea. The only tool we have to validate our mutual understanding of a given discourse is to engage in further discourse, a meta-discourse—a discourse about the previous discourse. We thus take a step up the ladder of abstraction. Our initial discourse was a tool for communicating certain ideas, feelings, and desires. That discourse now becomes the subject of a meta-discourse, and so on *ad infinitum.* In other words, just as absolute certainty of knowledge does not exist, neither does perfect communication.[16]

Also, we again have the phenomenon of convergence. Although our understanding of a given text will never be perfect, we can eliminate ambiguities, enlarge our understanding and thereby generate successively more accurate and more complete approximations to a perfect understanding. This process is called *explication,* meaning to *make explicit* that which was previously unclear or ambiguous. Just as there exists a whole gamut of epistemological methods, there are also established methods of explication, which will not be treated here in any detail.

Given the difficulties and limitations attending communication, one could make an *a priori* case that these difficulties are so great that intersubjective communication is practically impossible. This *existentialist fallacy* is the literary counterpart of total relativism in epistemology. It consists primarily in confusing understanding with explication, arriving at the conclusion that no text can be truly understood since no text can be totally explicated. Starting with the admitted fact that all communication is partial, it leaps to the false conclusion that communication is totally impossible (similar to the *some to all* leap of total relativism). We all have the feeling or sense that we communicate with each other, but, for those who fall victim to the existentialist fallacy, this is just an illusion. In their view, we are all alone, each enclosed in the cell of our subjectivity. This essential aloneness becomes, for them, the central fact of our existence.

The refutation of the existentialist fallacy is similar to the refutation of the fallacy of total relativism. In the latter case, we appealed to the observable success of scientific theories such as the Newton-Einstein theory of gravitation as incontrovertible evidence that science cannot reasonably be considered a cultural myth on a par with any other cultural myth. In the same way, we can point out the obvious fact that if communication were only an illusion, then society as we know it would not and could not exist. All of our higher-order social structures depend essentially (and demonstrably) on the fact that a significant degree of intersubjective communication is possible. Indeed, it is difficult to see how each generation of children could learn language if such communication were only an illusion.

There is an element of self-refutation in both deconstructionism and existentialism. In the first instance we put forth as a valid theory that there cannot be any valid theories. In the second instance, we expend great efforts in communicating to others that communication with others is impossible. Of course there are no absolutely valid theories and there is no perfect communication. The fallacy lies in taking these limitations to be the central reality rather than only a part of a larger and more adequate reality.

3. OBJECTIVITY IN COMMUNICATION

We have established beyond any reasonable doubt that significant intersubjective communication can and does exist. Against the background of this discussion, we now address assumption (3), which raises the question of the extent to which we can communicate objective knowledge of reality. On the one hand, we have a dialogue with objective reality which, under appropriate circumstances, generates a progressively more refined and accurate inner model of reality. On the other hand, we maintain an ongoing intersubjective dialogue in which we seek to communicate our point of view to others.

All communication seeks to fulfill some goal or purpose. Sometimes the goal is frankly and unashamedly subjective. We seek to share our thoughts, feelings, and desires to the maximum extent possible, within the context of whatever limitations are inherent in the communication process. This is maximalist communication and is epitomized by poetic language that makes liberal use of such devices as metaphor and multiple meanings.

At other times we seek to communicate as precisely as possible. This is minimalist language which renounces the use of metaphor and multiple meaning. It is epitomized by formal logical languages such as those used in programming and operating digital computers.

However, whatever may be the goal or intention of a given text, the fact remains that *all discourse emanates from a given point of view.* All text has an author, and the ideas expressed by the author cannot but reflect his or her understanding of reality. There is not, nor can there ever be, a totally *neutral* discourse, that is, a discourse which is wholly viewpoint-independent.

The question now arises of how to deal with viewpoint-dependency in our discourse about objective reality. This problem is similar to the problem of knower-reality interactions in connection with verifications, and the solution is likewise similar. We dealt with knower-reality interactions by making them explicit in our models. In the same way, we deal with viewpoint-dependency by making it explicit in our discourse.

We say that a discourse is *objective* to the degree that it makes explicit the (assumptions underlying the) viewpoint of its author. A discourse which refuses to acknowledge its viewpoint is *biased,* a discourse which gives no justification for its viewpoint is *dogmatic,* and a discourse which seeks to convey its viewpoint without making it explicit is *subjective.*

These definitions are important and deserve further discussion. A discourse consists of signs (expressions) and their meanings (interpretations). On one hand, signs are concrete entities, a part of observable, objective reality. On the other hand, interpretations are ideas and thus wholly subjective. Ontologically, a discourse is thus a hybrid, partly objective and partly subjective. It is therefore not in the ontological sense that we apply the predicate *objective* to a discourse. Applied to texts, objectivity relates both to the signs of the text and the possible meanings of the text. A text is objective if it makes certain affirmations about reality and, at the same time, incorporates certain affirmations about the relationship between the text and reality. We objectify a given discourse by extending it to include certain appropriate portions of its meta-discourse.

This definition of textual objectivity clarifies a major, ongoing misunderstanding about the nature of objectivity in discourse. Towards the beginning of the twentieth century, certain positivist philosophers of science advanced the notion that an author could achieve textual objectivity only by discoursing from a totally neutral, value-free, assumption-free viewpoint. However, subsequent developments in epistemology and linguistics made clear the point that we have already made in the above: there does not exist any such neutral viewpoint. Any point of view presupposes numerous assumptions.

Once the myth of viewpoint-neutrality was exploded, there were two responses in the philosophical community. The deconstructionists/postmodernists reacted by declaring that objectivity itself is a cultural myth (on a par with other cultural myths, of course). To strive for viewpoint neutrality is itself a value-choice—a viewpoint.

The other response is represented by the approach we have taken here of defining objectivity not as viewpoint-neutrality but rather as viewpoint-awareness. In this conception, we can all discourse objectively about anything and from any viewpoint. All we have to do is to become aware of our assumptions and to state them explicitly. This notion of objectivity is clearly coherent. The extent to which viewpoint-awareness is practically achievable is another question which we will discuss below.

In fact, the notion of objectivity as viewpoint-awareness is not new, and has a continuous history beginning at least as early as Euclid's *Elements*. This text makes a number of affirmations about geometrical figures and their spatial relationships. But it does more. To avoid subjective discussions of these affirmations, Euclid explicitly deduces them all from five explicit assumptions or axioms. The reader is free to reject Euclid's axioms if he so desires, but *if* he accepts them, then he cannot deny any of Euclid's further affirmations. Euclid has made his viewpoint totally explicit. Euclid's approach to objectivity in the *Elements* is known as the *axiomatic method* and it has played a prominent role in science and philosophy ever since.

Recall that we have defined reason as the process of becoming aware of our assumptions about reality (as opposed to common sense, which is prerational, and insanity, which is irrational). It is obvious that we cannot discourse objectively—in other words make our assumptions textually explicit—until we have made them explicit to ourselves. Thus, *textual objectivity is based on reason.* Objectivity and rationality go together. Textual objectivity is an expression of rationality.

Of course, we can choose reason without choosing textual objectivity. This is what creative artists do. They have become aware of their viewpoint but choose deliberately to write a subjective text in which they convey their viewpoint without making it explicit in the text itself. Their goal is to lead the reader to experience the author's viewpoint, without the reader necessarily becoming aware of the process that leads to the experience.

We are thus not making a value judgement that objective texts are in all circumstances superior to subjective texts. In each given instance, it depends on the goal or purpose of the discourse.

Another example of deliberately subjective discourse is *propaganda*, a rhetorical form whose purpose is to influence others towards the author's viewpoint but in ways that hide this intention. To be effective, propaganda cannot be objective. Propaganda is not irrational but antirational, the antithesis of rationality.

Socrates and Plato were the early champions of reason and Plato in particular took Euclid's *Elements* as the model of reason at its best. For Plato the goal of reason and objectivity was to ascend the ladder of abstraction towards a more adequate perception of the ultimate forms or first principles from which every lower thing was derived. Since reason involves increased self-awareness, this Platonic process cannot be achieved without a substantial degree of subjective self-development, leading to *wisdom,* which was for Plato the highest form of knowledge, objective or otherwise.

The modern positivist attempt to redefine objectivity as viewpoint-neutrality is something that Plato would have immediately denounced as a vain sophistry. Indeed, the modern positivist programme was consciously conceived in opposition to philosophical realism and, to some

extent, to metaphysics in general. Though differing from positivism in
many respects, deconstructionism and postmodernism share the positivist bias against realism and metaphysics, and this is why postmodernists
were so quick to use the generally recognized inadequacy of the positivist notion of objectivity-as-viewpoint-neutrality to formulate an attack
on objectivity and rationality itself in the form of total relativism.

4. THE EXTENT AND LIMITS OF OBJECTIVITY IN COMMUNICATION

In the preceeding section, we have clarified the nature and conception
of objectivity in communication: it is viewpoint-awareness and not viewpoint-neutrality. But to address adequately the problems raised by
assumption (3), we need to consider not just the possibility but the
practicality of achieving any significant degree of viewpoint-awareness.

Our example of the incommunicability of the subjective experience
of redness already shows that there are certain limits to the degree of
objectivity that can be attained in any discourse. We thus begin our
discussion by eliminating the possibility of absolute objectivity, just as
we have already eliminated absolutely adequate truth and absolutely
certain knowledge. We also reject as unreasonable the leap from relative
objectivity to total subjectivity. The reader should now be able to supply
the argument for himself or herself.[17]

More generally, a little reflection leads to the realization that total
viewpoint-awareness would amount to total self-awareness which is
clearly impossible. How indeed can our mind, which is only part of our
total self, completely encompass that self? Not only would we have to
become totally aware of such things as our unconscious thoughts and
autonomic nerve impulses, but the mind would have to encompass the
mind itself. This latter leads immediately to another infinite regress: the
mind would have to encompass itself, encompass itself encompassing
itself, etc., *ad infinitum*. The end (solution) to this infinite regress would
be a mind that is totally or absolutely aware of itself. Nothing in our
experience gives us any reasonable basis for believing that we humans
are capable of such total awareness.[18]

Thus, total objectivity in discourse would require total viewpoint-
awareness, which by definition is equivalent to the God-like quality of
absolute reason. Since these absolutes are, once again, impossible of

human attainment, the question then arises of the extent to which a high degree of relative objectivity can be attained. The answer, as we shall see, is quite a bit.

We begin with the extension, by definition, of the notion of truth to linguistic expressions. Until now the predicate *true* has applied to those parts of our inner model which reflect accurately some corresponding portion of reality. In other words, truth is the accuracy of the correspondence between reality and our inner model. By a *proposition* we mean any meaningful linguistic expression which makes affirmations about the way reality is structured. A typical example of a proposition would be any simple English sentence in the indicative mood, for example, "Grass is green."

It might seem at first than any meaningful linguistic expression would be a proposition, but that is too broad. Commands, "Go forth and multiply," and wishes, "I hope she loves me," are meaningful linguistic expressions but not propositions because they make no affirmation about how reality is in fact structured. A proposition is *true* if the state of affairs it affirms to be the case is in fact the case. Thus defined, truth is a function of two things: structure (of reality) and meaning (of the proposition).

We have already observed that meanings are partly syntactical (concrete and observable) and partly semantical (subjective and unobservable). The concrete part of meaning has to do with the syntactic structure of the proposition (e.g., the subject-predicate form of the proposition "Grass is green"). In its semantic aspect, meaning is a reflection of the inner model of the author of the discourse and, more generally, of the whole linguistic community associated with the given language. Meanings articulate our inner model.

There is thus a correspondence between our inner model and reality, on one hand, and a correspondence between our inner model and language, on the other hand. The difference is that we construct language but we do not construct the objective part of reality. Thus, a proposition is true if it correctly articulates an accurate inner model. A proposition will be false (untrue) either because it correctly articulates a false idea or else because it badly articulates a true idea.

Again, it is important to realize that a proposition may well be true without our knowing it to be so. "There is intelligent humanoid life on other planets" is a clear proposition whose truth or falsity is presently unknown to us. A proposition is true if it makes an accurate affirmation about the structure of reality; we may or may not be in a position to verify the accuracy of the given affirmation. This is essentially the distinction between truth and verification that we have already discussed in a preceeding section.

We need, now, to think about how propositions fare under changes of viewpoint. Since the grammar or syntax of a language is concrete and objective, it does not change with any change of viewpoint for grammatically correct speakers of the language. What can change is the interpretation of *lexicon:* you and I may, even unknowingly, attribute slightly different meanings to the same lexical terms. The proposition may then be true under my interpretation but false under yours.

Consider, for example, the statement: "You stepped on the little child's toy." There is a potential ambiguity as to whether it is the toy or the child that is little. In the first interpretation, I may be telling you that you stepped on the little toy of the child but not the big toy. In the second, I may be saying that you stepped on a toy (big or small) of the small child. Such ambiguities are not the only source of divergent interpretations, but they are a frequent source.

Ambiguities are usually clarified by enlarging the context. If you have just stepped on something and asked me whether it was the big toy or the little one, my statement now becomes unambiguous: it is the toy that is small. On the other hand, perhaps you have wondered which of two children, one big and one small, has had his toy stepped on.

A proposition is itself a discourse, and its context is simply a longer discourse in which the proposition is embedded. If the proposition is ambiguous when taken out of its context, then we must acknowledge that the proposition gets part of its meaning from its context. However, the meaning of the total discourse obviously depends on the meanings of the propositions it includes. This interplay between propositions and contexts gives rise to what is known as the *hermeneutic circle:* the meaning of a total context depends on the expressions that make it up and the meaning of an expression depends in part on its context.

In other words, meaning cannot be completely localized to a single expression but must be considered, to some extent, as distributed throughout a context. Nevertheless, in our ensuing discussion, we will make the simplifying assumption that propositions constitute independent, meaning-bearing expressions. In acknowledging this assumption, we are making our point of view explicit. In the light of the hermeneutic circle, we are therefore treating a somewhat idealized version of linguistic reality. However, experience has shown that the degree of idealization involved is not very great, especially with regard to the issue of objectivity in communication.

We now define the important notion of the objectivity of a proposition. A proposition is *objective* to the extent that its truth (or falsity) is invariant under changes of viewpoint. We now turn our attention to a special class of truths that are naturally invariant under changes of viewpoint, without our having to attain any viewpoint awareness whatever.

5. LOGICAL TRUTH, THE APOGEE OF PROPOSITIONAL OBJECTIVITY

A certain pattern has emerged from our various considerations in the foregoing. First, we address a philosophical notion such as truth, verification, objectivity, certainty, or communicability. We then discover that the notion is coherent but, disappointingly, relative. Of course, our disappointment is somewhat assuaged by the immense difference between *some* relativity and *total* relativity. Nevertheless our thirst for absolutes remains unsatisfied. Indeed, in the light of this recurrent pattern, it would be reasonable to conclude that we must abandon the search for absolutes of any kind. However, we now encounter a notion, *logical truth,* which surprisingly and satisfyingly does yield an absolute: absolute propositional objectivity. More precisely, the logical truths of a language (such as English) constitute a collection of propositions whose truth is absolutely objective (i.e., totally independent of viewpoint).

The definition is simple: a logical truth, of a given fixed language L, is a proposition of L that is true and which remains true under *all possible* lexical (re)interpretations (i.e., under *all possible* changes of viewpoint for grammatically correct speakers of L). This definition tells us the conditions a proposition must satisfy to be counted a logical truth. However the definition itself does not guarantee that there are in fact any such propositions. Indeed, it is initially hard to see how anything could remain invariant under such a broad range of changes of viewpoint.

The answer lies in the observation that the meaningful expressions of a language L are generated by two distinct kinds of syntactical expressions, the lexical and the logical. The lexicon comprises several *categories*, including all substantives (e.g., nouns, pronouns, nominal and pronominal phrases) and all predicates (e.g., verbs and predicate adjectives) except the copula of absolute identity. Logical expressions serve as *connectors* or *operators* which enable us to build propositions from lexical expressions and more complex propositions from simpler ones. In English, the main connectors (which we will call the *basic connectors*) are "not - - -", "if … then - - -", "… and - - -", "… or - - -", "… if and only if - - -", "… is the same as - - -", and the so-called *quantifiers,* "there is something such that [M]" and "for everything it is the case that [M]", where M is a meaningful expression. There are other connectors, but these will suffice since they constitute a *complete set* of connectors.[19]

Thus, any meaningful expression of a language L has an objective (syntactical) structure in terms of the operators used to build it up, starting with simple predicates and substantives. This structure determines the *grammatical (or logical) form* of the given expression. When we reinterpret only elements of the lexicon of an expression, we do not change its logical form. In other words, logical form does not vary under changes of viewpoint (again, among grammatical speakers of the language L). It follows that every proposition P that has the same logical form as some logical truth is itself a logical truth. Logical truth is preserved under similarity of logical form.[20]

Let us illustrate with the simplest example, the *is* of identity. Suppose I ask you whether or not the proposition "John is the author of the newspaper article" is true. You will answer that you cannot know until I tell you which person named *John* I am referring to and which newspaper article I am talking about. In other words, you need to know some facts about my viewpoint in order to determine the truth or falsity of the proposition. Now, let us substitute in the proposition the substantive *John* for the nominal phrase "the author of the newspaper article". After the substitution is made, we obtain the proposition "John is John". If now, I ask you whether or not the proposition "John is John" is true, you can answer immediately with a resounding and emphatic *yes*. Of course you still don't know which John I am referring to, but now it no longer matters, because every existing entity is identical with itself. (Here, as always, we assume that every occurrence of a fixed proper noun within a given discourse has the same referant or denotation.) "John is John" is thus a logical truth of the English language.

More generally, we can say that any proposition having the form "A is A", where A is any substantive, is a logical truth. Using one of our quantifiers, we can also affirm as a logical truth that "For everything x, x is x." In other words, everything that exists is identical with itself.[21]

Another simple example would be the proposition: "If it is raining today, then it is raining today." Again, "it is raining today" will be true or false depending on who says it, where and when. Its truth is viewpoint-dependent. But, "If it is raining today, then it is raining today" will always be true regardless of the truth or falsity of the proposition "it is raining today." It is true no matter who says it or under what circumstances it is said. It is invariant under any possible change of viewpoint among grammatically correct speakers of the English language (because all such speakers will keep the same logical meaning of the connector "if ... then - - -").[22]

The reason for this last condition now becomes fully apparent. In determining logical truth, we are free to reinterpret lexical expressions but not operational expressions. No grammatical speaker of the language will change the meaning of the connectors, because their meaning is fixed by the very rules of grammar that the speaker is bound to observe (by virtue of being a grammatical speaker of the language).

In other words: grammar, and the meaning of grammatical operators, are entirely concrete and objective. These meanings are defined operationally. They do not depend in any way on the viewpoint of the speaker (i.e., on the inner model of any subject). Grammar is the formal aspect of language, the part that is pure form, totally objective, totally explicit. Yet, when combined appropriately with lexical expressions, grammatical form contributes to the meaning of the whole expression.[23]

Notice that logical truth is defined with respect to (relative to) a given language. It is therefore not a translinguistic notion. However, because grammatical form can be made totally explicit, the logical truths of a given language are determined absolutely (i.e., totally objectively).[24]

In contrast to grammatical meaning, lexical meaning is not totally explicit, because it cannot be defined in purely operational terms. Thus, the lack of total objectivity in communication generally, as well as the hermeneutic circle, derive from the relative (but irreducible) subjectivity of lexical meaning.

6. RELATIONAL LOGIC VS. ATTRIBUTIONAL LOGIC

Logical truths are those truths that are truth-invariant under all changes of viewpoint that conserve logical form (all purely lexical reinterpretations). Logical falsity is another invariant notion. A proposition is logically false if it is false and remains false under all purely lexical reinterpretations. The *negation* "Not P" of any logically false proposition P is logically true, and vice-versa. Logical truth and logical falsity are properties of propositions of a given language L—properties that either hold or do not hold for a given proposition P of L.[25]

More generally, a property is a *one-place* predicate (or attribute) such as "… is big" , "… is true", "… is green." Thus, an attribute expresses some quality that either holds or does not hold for any given (single) object. Aristotle's system of logic, frequently called *syllogism,* was capable of dealing only with properties.

However, modern logic is capable of dealing with *relations* (i.e., with predicates (attributes) that may have any (finite) number of *places*). For example, a binary (two-place) predicate would be "… is bigger than - - -" or "… is a brother of - - -". A three-place predicate would be betweenness: "… is between - - - and # # #". Thus, a relation expresses a link or connection that either holds or does not hold between two or more objects (or between a given object and itself).

The development of a *logic of relations* was only begun in the latter part of the nineteenth century, and completed in the twentieth century. It turns out that this logic (also called *predicate logic*) is much more powerful and flexible than Aristotle's syllogism, while including the latter as a special case (as the predicate logic of unary predicates or attributes).

The greater generality of relational logic with respect to Aristotle's logic of attributes brings with it greater power as well. Indeed, the logical truths of purely attributional logic can be seen to be *computationally decidable.* This means that there exists a computer algorithm which will accept any statement of attributional logic and terminate in a finite number of steps giving an output of *1* if the statement is a logical truth and *0* if it is not. We can thus program a computer to detect all and only logical truths of attributional logic.

However, it is now known (see note 24) that no such algorithm can exist for the logical truths of relational logic, though these latter are *semidecidable.* This means that there exists a computer algorithm with the following properties: the algorithm will accept any statement of relational logic. If the algorithm terminates (in a finite number of steps), then the statement is certainly a logical truth (of relational logic). However, if the algorithm does not terminate (and it may not), we cannot conclude that the statement is not a logical truth. We simply do not know.

Semidecidability is like those irritating medical tests which, when they come back positive, mean that you definitely have the illness, but if they return negative, do not allow us to conclude that you do not have the illness. You still might have the illness.

7. ARTICULATING LOGICAL TRUTH: LOGICAL IMPLICATION AND LOGICAL DEDUCTION

We want now to take a definite step up the "ladder of abstraction" and make language itself the object of our discourse. We will thus be *talking about talking*—discoursing about discourse. Language will thus be both the object of our discourse (sometimes called the *object language*) and the medium in which we discourse (the so-called *metalanguage*). These two languages may well overlap to a large extent, or even be identical. But we must carefully distinguish their roles relative to each other in any given context if we are to avoid confusion.

A useful analogy is thinking about thinking. I may use my brain to study my own brain. My brain as an object of study (a grey mass of neuronal cells connected to each other) will appear quite different to me than my brain as experienced (as thoughts, feelings, intuitions, or mental images). The first case would be the brain as object language and the second the brain as metalanguage.

In order to objectify our discussion of language, we will have recourse to the use of schematic letters, primarily in referring to various expressions in the object language. Such devices may seem unnatural at first, but the clarifying advantages of this approach soon become evident. Indeed, our discussion of the object language will be focused almost exclusively on the grammatical and logical form of expressions rather than on their content. Using schematic letters allows us to consider the form in abstraction from any specific (and thus distracting) content.

Let us give a simple example. We will henceforth symbolize the conditional connector "if ... then - - -" by use of the horseshoe symbol

⊃, giving "... ⊃ - - -". Thus, the vernacular statement "If I have a fever, then I am sick" can be symbolized: (I have a fever)⊃(I am sick). Now, if we go further, letting the schematic letter P represent "I have a fever" and Q "I am sick", then we can represent the original proposition by the schematic form (P⊃Q). Suppose that, at this point, I proceed to take my temperature and find that I do indeed have a fever. Thus, P is true. Since (P⊃Q) is likewise true, it now follows that Q is true.

This obviously holds for any propositions having the requisite formal relationship with each other. That is, for any propositions P and Q whatever, if (P⊃Q) is true and if, further, P is true, then Q is true. This is a universal rule of predicate logic, the rule known as *Modus Ponens*. Such a formal rule of logic is often itself stated in schematic form as follows:

$$\frac{P, (P{\supset}Q)}{Q}$$

This would be read as: "For any propositions P and Q, whenever the two *hypotheses* P and (P⊃Q) above the line are true, then the *conclusion* Q below the the line is also true." We say the rule is *formal* because it only depends on the (logical) form of the propositions, not on their specific (lexical) content.

Such a rule gives us the *right* to infer or deduce that the conclusion (below the line) is true whenever the hypotheses (above the line) hold. A formal rule therefore establishes a relation between propositions of a particular form. For example, *Modus Ponens* involves a three-place relationship M which holds between any three propositions of the form P, (P⊃Q), and Q respectively. More formally, we would say that three propositions P, X, and Q are in the relation M, symbolically, M(P, X, Q) holds, if and only if X = (P⊃Q). In this case, the latter proposition is true whenever the first two are (the rule of *Modus Ponens*).

We want now to focus on binary relations between propositions of a fixed language L. Examples would be "... is longer than - - -" or "... is more (grammatically) complex than - - -". Such statements of relations between propositions of the object language L actually occur in the metalanguage of L. It is important not to confuse relations between propositions of L (which give rise to statements in the metalanguage) with logical operators such as " if... then ...", that occur within the object language L itself.

Let us elaborate on this briefly. As we have seen above, the binary logical operator ⊃ combines with two propositions P and Q of a given language L to yield another (more complex) proposition (P⊃Q) of the language L. A relation between propositions of L is a predicate *in the metalanguage of* L which applies to two propositions P and Q of L to form a statement (proposition) within the metalanguage of L—the meta-discourse *about* L. Such a relation is thus a predicate (lexical element) of the metalanguage of L. Thus, the statement S that "P is longer than Q", where P and Q are L-propositions, is itself a proposition of the metalanguage of L.

The statement S *could* also be a proposition of L, but only if the predicate *longer than* is part of the *lexicon* of L. (Remember that object language and metalanguage can overlap.) However, in no case whatever can a *predicate* of a language L be a *logical operator* of L (remember that lexical elements and logical operators constitute two distinct, non-intersecting categories of syntactical expressions). In other words, a logical operator such as ⊃ is used to build propositions of L from other propositions of L, while a relation between propositions of L gives rise to a proposition in the metalanguage about L.

We can however use binary logical operators in the object language, together with properties (attributes) defined in the metalanguage, to define binary relations in the metalanguage. The simplest and most important example is the relationship of *logical implication,* symbolized by the double-bodied arrow ⇒. We now use the conditional connector ⊃ of the object language and the attribute of logical truth (defined in the metalanguage) to define the binary relationship of implication ⇒.

Given two L-propositions P and Q, the L-proposition "If P then Q" is called the *conditional* with P as *antecedent* and Q as *consequent.* We say (in the metalanguage), of two L-propositions P and Q, that P *implies* Q, and we write P⇒Q, if the conditional (P⊃Q) is logically true. With a little extra symbolism, we can neatly schematize this statement. Where P is any L-proposition, we write (in the metalanguage) ⊢P to mean "P is a logical truth." By definition, P⇒Q means "'If P then Q' is logically true", now symbolized by ⊢(P⊃Q). Thus, even more succinctly: P⇒Q if and only if ⊢(P⊃Q). We have thus used the binary logical connector ⊃ of the object language together with the unary predicate (attribute) "⊢..." of the metalanguage to define the binary relation "... ⇒ - - -" of the metalanguage.

To see clearly what this means, we first observe that the conditional (P⊃Q) is true if either P is false or Q is true. In other words, to say that the truth of Q is conditional upon (or relative to) the truth of P is to say that Q cannot be false if P is true. To say that a conditional "If P then Q" is logically true is thus to say that *every* reinterpretation of lexicon that makes the antecedent P true also makes the consequent Q true, or equivalently, that any lexical reinterpretation that falsifies Q must also falsify P, or again equivalently, that there is no single lexical interpretation that satisfies P while falsifying Q (see note 25 for elaboration on terminology).

In particular, if Q is logically true then it is absolutely true (unfalsifiable) and thus true relative to any other proposition P. So a logically true proposition is implied by any proposition. Similarly, if P is logically false then it is unsatisfiable and thus implies any other proposition Q. These are, of course, trivial instances of logical implication.

There is one more trivial case worth mentioning. Suppose that P and Q have no lexical elements in common. Suppose, further, that P is satisfiable (not logically false) and Q falsifiable (not logically true). Then P cannot imply Q, because an interpretation of that part of the L-lexicon which actually occurs in P puts no conditions whatsoever on the interpretation of the lexical elements that occur in Q. Thus, in this case, we can easily construct an interpretation of the lexical expressions of the language L that satisfies P while falsifying Q.

Just as for logical truth, the general case for logical implication cannot be mechanically decided. Precisely, this means it is possible that, for some L-propositions P and Q, P⇒Q holds even though we never succeed in discovering this fact. However, there does exist a finite set of purely syntactical *rules of logic* that is *complete* in the following sense: if P⇒Q does in fact hold, then Q can be obtained from P by some finite sequence of applications of the logical rules. In this case, we say that we have *deduced* Q from P, and we write P⊢Q. Using this terminology, we can state the completeness property more succinctly: If P implies Q (thus, (P⊃Q) is logically true), then we can deduce Q from P, P⊢Q. Let us state this in the form of a schematic rule (similar to *Modus Ponens*):

$$\frac{P \Rightarrow Q}{P \vdash Q}$$

The rules of logical deduction are purely formal (syntactical) and concrete. As a consequence, we can decide absolutely (mechanically and objectively), for any given finite set K of L-expressions $\{S_1, S_2, ..., S_n\}$, whether or not a given L-expression S_{n+1}, follows from K by some application of the rules. We can also decide, for any given finite *sequence* $S_1 S_2 ... S_n$ of expressions, whether, for each i, $1 \leq i < n$, S_{i+1} follows from the previous $S_1, ..., S_i$ by our deductive rules. If this is the case, then we say that the sequence is a *deductive sequence* or a *valid deduction*. A deductive sequence with $S_1 = P$ and $S_n = Q$, is a *deduction of Q from P* or (*a proof of Q from P*). To assert that $P \vdash Q$ holds is precisely to say that there does exist a valid deduction of P from Q.

Thus, it is decidable whether a given sequence of expressions of L is or is not a valid deduction, but not whether there *exists* a deduction of a given Q from a given P (i.e., that $P \vdash Q$ holds). In other words: there is no absolutely certain method of finding a valid deduction, but there is an absolutely certain method of verifying that a given sequence is a valid deduction.

The reciprocal of completeness is called *soundness,* and is also true: If Q can be deduced from P by our logical rules, $P \vdash Q$, then P does in fact imply Q, $P \Rightarrow Q$. Putting soundness and completeness together, we thus have the following equivalence: P *implies* Q *if and only if there exists a valid deduction of Q from P; symbolically,* $P \Rightarrow Q$ *(equivalently $\vdash (P \supset Q)$) if and only if* $P \vdash Q$.

The soundness of our rules follows from the fact that they preserve satisfaction under any given lexical interpretation. Thus, suppose $P \vdash Q$. If, now, P is satisfied by a given lexical interpretation I, then Q is also satisfied by I. Since this holds for every possible lexical interpretation, then $P \Rightarrow Q$ by definition. In particular, whatever is deduced from true propositions is true and whatever is deduced from logically true propositions is logically true.

This gives rise to several variant forms of the *Modus Ponens* rule, each with its strengths and weaknesses. We write each of these variants in schematic form:

(1) $\dfrac{P, P \Rightarrow Q}{Q}$ or equivalently $\dfrac{P, P \vdash Q}{Q}$ or equivalently $\dfrac{P, \vdash (P \supset Q)}{Q}$

Notice that if, in the above schemata, we strengthen the hypothesis P to the stronger hypothesis ⊢P, then we can also strengthen the conclusion from Q to ⊢Q, yielding the scheme:

(II)
$$\frac{\vdash P, \ \vdash(P{\supset}Q)}{\vdash Q}$$

For ease of reference, we also restate the original form of *Modus Ponens:*

(III)
$$\frac{P, \ (P{\supset}Q)}{Q}$$

In this case, we get the conclusion Q with a weaker hypothesis, (P⊃Q).

In practice, (I) is generally more useful than (III) for reaching the simple conclusion that Q holds, and it is helpful to see why. In applying the form (III) of *Modus Ponens,* we must know that (P⊃Q) holds, which means we must know either that P is false or that Q is true. But since we also assume P, P cannot be false, and so Q must be known to be true in order for (P⊃Q) to be true. Thus, the very act of verifying the two hypotheses amounts to knowing that Q is true, which is the conclusion we are seeking. In other words, if the truth of Q is not in doubt, then we can immediately affirm Q without having to appeal to hypotheses regarding P and the connection between P and Q.

Thus, the context in which *Modus Ponens* is most frequently applied is when we seek to establish the truth of Q precisely because it is in doubt. The usual strategy is to find some P whose truth we know, and then to find a deduction of Q from P, thus verifying the hypothesis P⊢Q. The conclusion that Q is true is now truly novel information.

Interestingly and importantly: even though our logical rules are themselves obvious, they do not preserve obviousness, because to determine whether P⊢Q (and thus P⇒Q) holds, we must show there *exists* some valid deduction of Q from P, and this is undecidable as we have seen. However, every step of a logical proof is obvious, because we can determine absolutely and objectively (mechanically) whether or not that step is justified by our rules. Thus, P may be obviously (even trivially) true, and the proof of Q from P may be obvious (once we have found it), but Q, though now known to be true, may not be obviously true at all.

Thus, the power of predicate logic is that it enables us *to derive the unobvious from the obvious in a finite number of individually obvious steps.* Herein lies the value of logic and the justification for the central role it plays in the methodology of minimalism. If logic derived only the obvious from the obvious, it would be useless. This would likewise be the case if logic only derived the unobvious from the unobvious (and certainly if it derived the obvious from the unobvious). As we will see in the following section, the power of logic to derive the unobvious from the obvious increases immeasurably the quantity of information that can be objectively communicated.

The establishment of a complete and sound set of rules for predicate logic has been one of the major intellectual achievements of the twentieth century. Indeed, the conception, construction, and implementation of electronic digital computers all make essential use of the logic of relations. As 'Abdu'l-Bahá has stated:

> *Know then, with regard to the mathematical sciences, that it was only in this distinguished age, this great century, that their scope was widened, their unresolved difficulties solved, their rules systematized, and their diversity realized. The discoveries made by earlier philosophers and the views they held were not established upon a firm basis or a sound foundation for they wished to confine the worlds of God within the smallest compass and narrow limit and were quite unable to conceive what lay beyond...*[26]

Notice that 'Abdu'l-Bahá identifies one of the major limitations of classical philosophy as its inability or refusal to deal adequately with the notion of infinity. If reality is indeed infinite, as 'Abdu'l-Bahá affirms here and elsewhere, then the *a priori* exclusion of such notions as infinite regresses guarantees that our models will be severely inadequate. Moreover, such exclusions were made not for any logical reasons but simply because of the difficulty of the human mind to *conceive* of an infinity. This is essentially a form of subjectivism—that what we cannot conceive doesn't exist. It confuses our subjective ideas about reality with reality itself; it confuses the map with the territory.

8. OBJECTIVITY IN COMMUNICATION REVISITED: THE AXIOMATIC METHOD

Earlier on, we established that objectivity is properly understood as viewpoint-awareness rather than viewpoint-neutrality. It follows that I can communicate objectively with you to the degree that I can convey to you my viewpoint. Of course, we know in advance that it is not possible to convey the totality of my viewpoint, because that presupposes the impossible condition of total self-awareness.

However it is possible that a certain part of my inner model can be made explicit and objectively conveyed to you. In particular, those aspects of my inner model which can be formulated as objective propositions can certainly be conveyed. However, an essential precondition for objective communication is what may be called the *will to truth* on the part of both participants in the dialogue. Our goal must be to clarify, not to persuade.

First, I must be willing to acknowledge that a given proposition P accurately reflects a part of my inner model. This, of course, is just a convoluted way of saying that I recognize that I truly believe P. Notice that, here, we do not get into any problems of verification. I don't claim that I have verified P, only that I believe it to be true. There is an immense difference between knowing what is in fact the case and knowing what I believe to be the case. A minimum of self-insight is all that is necessary for the latter. So, the first step in objective communication is the objective articulation of belief.

However, once committed to a given set of beliefs, $P_1, ..., P_n$, I am also committed to all of the logical consequences of these beliefs, in other words, to every proposition that is logically implied by the *conjunction* of the P_i (i.e., the proposition $(P_1 \& P_2 \& ... \& P_n)$).[27] Of course, neither you nor I may know initially whether a given proposition Q is indeed a logical consequence of the P_i, but we both do know that when and if we find a deduction of Q from $(P_1 \& P_2 \& ... \& P_n)$, then by the *Modus Ponens* rule, I am as committed to belief in Q as I am to any of the P_i.

Such a deduction may be made either by you or by me. It will be made by me primarily to justify that my belief in Q is consistent with and flows from my belief in the P_i. However, your motivation in making the deduction might well be to show me that the highly unreasonable proposition Q is in fact a consequence of the P_i, the obvious point being that I must seriously revise my commitment to at least one of the P_i in order to avoid commitment to the troublesome Q.

The most troublesome case of all is when Q is a *logical contradiction* (i.e., a logical falsity of the form "P and not-P", symbolized by $(P\&(\neg P))$).[28] If such a contradiction can be deduced from the P_i, then the set $\{P_1, ..., P_n\}$ is *inconsistent* in the precise sense that the P_i cannot be together (simultaneously) true under any lexical interpretation whatever (which is equivalent to saying that the conjunction $(P_1 \& P_2 \& ... \& P_n)$ is logically false).

The reciprocal of the above also holds. That is: if the set $\{P_1, ..., P_n\}$ is inconsistent, then there does exist an explicit deduction of a contradiction $(P\&(\neg P))$ from the P_i. This follows immediately from the completeness of our logical rules.[29]

Thus, inconsistency reduces to logical falsehood, which, like logical truth, cannot be computationally decided. The fact that we have not yet deduced a contradiction from a given set of beliefs does not mean that the beliefs are consistent. We may just not have been clever enough to have found a deduction of a contradiction. Hence, a set of beliefs may be logically inconsistent without our ever discovering it to be so.[30]

Again, the presumption is that, in our dialogue, we are both seeking the truth. If that is indeed the case, then I will be just as happy (or unhappy) whether it is you or I who proves my beliefs inconsistent. If my beliefs are in fact inconsistent, then that fact is a truth that I want to know.

Of course, in practice things rarely proceed in this manner. If we are each seeking not truth but to persuade the other of our viewpoint (to *win the argument*), then we will not seek to clarify our respective positions (for fear of falling into unforeseen contradiction), but rather to criticize the other's position while disclosing as little as possible of our own. We will each focus upon and attack the weakest points of the other's belief system. In this case there will be little objectivity in communication because we are not seeking objectivity.[31]

The prevalence of disputation, aggressivity, and confrontation in intersubjective dialogue has led to the popular notion that "it is impossible to be objective," meaning not just that our egotistic human nature defeats objectivity, but that it is even logically impossible to have an objective dialogue or discourse. But, as we have seen, there is no logical or linguistic barrier whatsoever to objectivity. We can always choose to communicate with perfect objectivity, but we both must have the will to do so—to make our viewpoint explicit. It is true, however, that objectivity in communication does not happen automatically.

Let us sum up. Objectivity is viewpoint-awareness not viewpoint-neutrality. Objectivity in discourse can be obtained by first formulating a certain part of our inner model in the form of objective propositions, and then explicitly deducing other propositions from the initial ones. Thus, there can still be doubt as to whether the initial propositions are true, but no doubt as to the fact that the author holds them (and hence their logical consequences) to be true. The author has completely conveyed (that given part of) his point of view to the reader.

This form of discourse is called the *axiomatic method,* and it was used by Euclid in writing his *Elements.* Starting with only five initial propositions (called *axioms*), Euclid gives explicit deductions for hundreds of propositions (called *theorems)* about geometrical figures. One can call into question the truth of Euclid's axioms, but not the fact that the theorems are all implied by the axioms, because this is shown explicitly. This complete objectivity of deductive truth has been recognized explicitly by 'Abdu'l-Bahá in the following passage, among others:

> *Know then that those mathematical questions which have stood the test of scrutiny and about the soundness of which there is no doubt are those that are supported by incontrovertible and logically binding proofs and by the rules of geometry as applied to astronomy … .*[32]

'Abdu'l-Bahá's reference to the application to astronomy of the rules of geometry almost certainly refers to Newton's *Principia,* the second most historically significant use of the axiomatic method. In that work, Newton deduces the observed laws of planetary motion from essentially five explicit axioms.

Thus, the axiomatic method provides an eveready framework or paradigm for objective discourse, whenever there is the will to objectivity.

The axiomatic method is useful for truth-seeking (our dialogue with reality) as well as for objectivity in communication (our dialogue with each other). The organization of (a part of) a personal belief system in axiomatic form, where most of one's beliefs are deduced from a few axiomatic ones, has the effect of *localizing* questions of truth and verification to the axioms themselves. If we have established, by logical deduction, that P implies Q, then any empirical verification of the truth of P immediately transfers to Q. We do not have to worry about a separate empirical verification for Q.

In an axiomatic system (also called an axiomatic *theory*), every theorem is true, relative to the truth of the axioms. Thus, for such a system, all the problems inherent in the verification process (which we have discussed in the foregoing) can be localized to the axioms: the theorems automatically inherit the degree of empirical verification of the axioms.

This is an extremely important point, because some philosophers have tried to separate completely the empirical and the logical, holding that all propositions must be empirically verified independently (if at all), and that logic serves only as a kind of word game to organize the body of empirical truths in a useful way. However, our analysis has shown that logical truth is empirically grounded and inseparable from empirical truth.[33]

Suppose, then, that we are given an accumulated body of (relatively) verified truths. We can discover new truth in essentially one of three ways. We can empirically verify a new proposition Q which was previously unverified. This could be the result of new experimental techniques or just new experiences of reality (e.g., sending a probe to a distant planet for the first time). Or, we can discover that the proposition Q is logically implied by other previously validated truths. Thus, *we can in fact discover new empirical truths by purely logical means, without any immediate recourse to new experience.* Of course, in this case the empirical verification of Q will be inherited, by deduction, from the ultimate empirical verifications on which the whole system rests.[34]

In the third instance, we may encounter a clear empirical refutation of a proposition Q which was already part of our system. We now have new knowledge (i.e., that what we thought to be a truth is in fact a falsehood). We will of course respond to this new knowledge by removing Q from our system. But what if Q is logically implied by other propositions of our system? Then other propositions will also have to go. The extent of damage done to a system by a strong empirical refutation of only one proposition can sometimes be extensive.

Refutation can occur in another way, namely by the deduction of a logical contradiction (P&(¬P)) from some finite set of propositions of the system. This tells us that our system as a whole is inconsistent, and means that at least one of the propositions of the system will have to be discarded. This, again, is new knowledge.[35]

Thus, the knowledge-seeking enterprise is carried forward neither by logic alone nor by experience alone, but by an appropriate combination of both. Moreover, in moving forward from the known to the unknown, we must be able to conceive of not only what is true but also what *may be* true. This involves great use of intuition and the creative imagination. After all, we cannot apply either empirical or logical tests until an appropriate proposition has been formulated!

IV. REDUCTIONISM, SUBJECTIVISM, AND MINIMALISM

I. THE EXTENT AND LIMITS OF OBJECTIFICATION

We now enter into one of the major minefields of contemporary philosophy: the axiomatic method gives us the means for prosecuting an objective discourse, but does not tell us what can or cannot be objectified (made explicit in discourse). Among the possible answers to this question, there are two extreme positions.

The first is rationalistic or objectivistic reductionism, which says that everything can be objectified (the strong reductionist thesis) or at least that whatever cannot be objectified is worthless or meaningless (the weak reductionist thesis). The other extreme position holds that to objectivize is to trivialize: the only really significant aspects of our inner model are so subjective they can never be objectified. Each of these positions will be discussed in turn.

A reductionist will of course acknowledge, if pushed a bit, that there are certain emotions, feelings, or intuitions that cannot be objectified. But the reductionist will regard these not just as transrational, but as *irrational*. If we take rationality to be the essence of the human, then the irrational is, in some sense, nonhuman or antihuman (or, perhaps, subhuman).

We have already seen that rationality is a precondition to objectivity, but we have never claimed that rationality *reduces* to objectivity. However, the reductionist tends to consider that everything rational is, in principle, objectifiable, thereby equating the rational with the objective. Thus, anything that is irreducibly subjective—that resists objectification—is, from his standpoint, both irrational and subhuman.

Let us consider, for example, a typical reductionist view of the incommunicability of the subjective sensation of redness, which we discussed in an earlier section on limitations in intersubjective communication. We can give an objective definition of the color *red* in terms of measured emissions on a spectrograph. We can then say that, since almost all normal subjects will give essentially the same protocol as a function of this definition (i.e., they will spontaneously classify as red precisely those objects spectrographically measured to be so), then whatever experience is not captured by this objective definition is just so much inner trash. It has no objective existence and thus no real existence. In this way, objectivistic reductionism tends to equate realness with objectivity.

Reductionism is thus behavioristic and operationalistic. For the strict reductionist, all meaning is operational (and thus objective, concrete, and observable). Logical meaning is indeed purely operational, as we have seen above. However, the reductionist believes that *all* meaning, including lexical meaning, is ultimately operational: lexical terms are either spurious, or else they have an operational meaning that we have not yet learned how to objectify.

Many reductionists are also materialists, believing that operational and logical meaning can itself be explained in terms of the observable neurological configuration of the physical brain and nervous system. Thus, strict reductionism tends to identify the human, the rational, the real, the objective, the operational, the observable, and the material. By logical negation, it also tends thereby to identify the subhuman, the irrational, the unreal (imaginary), the subjective, the abstract, the unobservable, and the spiritual.

In refuting reductionism, perhaps the best way to start is with the very precise observation that *objectivity is itself the product of human subjectivity.* We can successfully objectify a certain part of our inner model only because we, as human subjects, can presume a vast (subjective) context of intuitively understood meanings, feelings, thoughts, intuitions, and desires. These spiritual capacities of the human being all derive from our *consciousness (self-awareness),* which creates the inner, subjective world from which language, logic, and rationality all emerge. Had we not this vast and rich conscious subjectivity, we would not be able to achieve the very viewpoint-awareness that constitutes objectivity in the first place.

The reductionist, then, is looking at objectivity only as a finished *product,* and he is thereby neglecting the whole *process* which has been necessary to produce this product. In declaring human subjectivity to be, in some sense, unreal, he has defined essential humanity out of existence.

Further, it is gratuitous and arbitrary to declare what lies beyond objectivity and/or reason to be *ir*rational. Undoubtedly there are indeed irrational and subrational elements to human subjectivity, but why can there not also be *trans*rational elements to our subjectivity—aspects of our inner experience which go beyond the rational without contradicting the rational? Why is it necessary to see such things as intuition or mystic experience as against rationality instead of adjuncts to rationality which can indeed illumine reason? In this regard, 'Abdu'l-Bahá has said that reason alone is like a perfect mirror in a dark room—a mirror which can serve its purpose only when illumined by the light of inner experience:

> *The human spirit which distinguishes man from the animal is the rational soul.... . It is like a mirror which, although clear, polished and brilliant, is still in need of light. Until a ray of the sun reflects upon it, it cannot discover the heavenly secrets.*[36]

It is irrational in itself to assume, without justification, that whatever lies beyond the rational and objective is necessarily lesser. Indeed, it is much more reasonable on the face of it to assume that a human subjectivity capable of producing rationality must itself be, in some sense, greater than its own product.

And look what is declared by the reductionist to be irrelevant emotional trash: not only our experience of redness, but our experience of love, of beauty, of communion with God—all the incomparable richness of human subjectivity.

However, as it turns out, the pursuit of objectivity and the axiomatic method has itself led to the ultimate and definitive refutation of reductionism—Gödel's incompleteness theorem. Our discussion here would be inadequate without some attempt to explicate the philosophical import of this central result of modern logic.

2. INDETERMINACY, GÖDEL'S THEOREM

Gallileo said that nature was writ in the language of mathematics. Mathematical language puts a premium on exactness and precision of expression. Ideally, a mathematical language is totally formalizable in such manner that every grammatically well-formed expression has only one logical meaning. In this sense, mathematical language is *linear:* text (syntax) is already linear, and if we avoid metaphor and multiple meaning in our lexicon, then our semantics will also be linear. In this case, each syntactical sign *is* its own meaning. It is precisely such totally linearized languages that are used, for example, in computer programming. Indeed, the only *meaning* that a computer can attribute to a symbol is the symbol itself, because the computer has no subjectivity.

Following Galileo, Descartes conceived of the vast philosophic enterprise of generating a complete description of the whole of reality in exact, mathematical terms. Moreover, Descartes took concrete steps towards the fulfillment of this programme by inventing algebraic geometry, which, for the first time in history, allowed a quantitative treatment of spatial intuition. Still, for most philosophers, Descartes' daring rationalistic dream appeared too ambitious to be workable.

However, these perceptions began to change when Isaac Newton published his *Principia* in which he did in fact deduce virtually all of the science then known from a few objective principles. Moreover, Newton and Leibniz independently invented calculus, which raised the power and broadened the extent of mathematical language to an unprecedented degree. And Newton's theory worked. Now the doubters of Descartes' dream were on the defensive, and materialism, mechanism, rationalism, and objectivism were in the ascendancy.

When, in the nineteenth century, Darwin's theory of evolution held forth the possibility of explaining life itself in objective and rational terms, the triumph of Cartesianism seemed imminent. The first cracks in objectivism appeared with the development of quantum mechanics by Bohr, Heisenberg, Dirac, and others in the 1920's. For the first time, probabilities, and thus uncertainties, were introduced in an essential way into the hardest of physical theories. More particularly, Heisenberg's uncertainty principle showed that it was impossible—at least within the established mathematical framework of quantum mechanics—to describe simultaneously (make explicit) both the position and the velocity of an electron.

The indeterminacy principle was not a definitive refutation of Cartesianism, because it did not exclude the logical possibility that some other formal language could be found in which this indeterminacy did not occur. Nevertheless it certainly did refute the universality of the existing language, and without suggesting any natural alternative.

The definitive refutation of Cartesianism came in 1931 with the advent of Gödel's theorem, which deals with theories in general, not just particular physical theories. For a proper understanding and articulation of Gödel's result, we need to state a few further definitions related to axiomatic theories.

An axiomatic system T is *complete* if it deductively decides every proposition. Precisely, this means that, for every proposition P in the language L, either P is a theorem of T or else ¬P is a theorem of T. If T is incomplete, then there has to be at least one proposition P which is not deductively determined (i.e., such that neither P nor ¬P is a theorem of T). But, one of P or ¬P has to be true! Thus, if T is incomplete, then there must be truths in the language L that are not provable in T.

Notice that, trivially, any inconsistent system is complete (and thus any incomplete system consistent). However, the only interesting complete systems are the consistent ones.

An axiomatic system is *objectively specifiable* if each of its axioms can be explicitly designated. Until now, we have only considered axiomatic theories with a finite number of axioms. Such theories are certainly objectively specifiable, but there are in fact objectively specifiable theories with an infinity of axioms.

Finally, an axiomatic system T in a language L is *sufficiently rich* if L contains the basic lexicon of arithmetic and if the axioms of T contain the basic axioms of arithmetic. This condition is quite weak, and would certainly have to be satisfied by any axiomatic theory that claimed to describe all of reality,

Now, Gödel's theorem establishes that *any consistent, objectively specifiable, sufficiently rich axiomatic theory T is incomplete.* Thus, there will be propositions P in the language L such that neither P nor ¬P are theorems of T. This means that there are true propositions in L that cannot be proved in T.

It might appear at first that we could overcome Gödel incompleteness of a consistent theory T simply by adding, as new axioms, enough of the true but unprovable propositions of L to form a complete theory T'. However, this strategy founders on the following dilemma. If, on one hand, the new axioms are all explicitly given, then the new theory T' will itself be objectively specifiable and certainly, as an extension of T, sufficiently rich (and consistent, since we have added only true propositions). Thus, by Gödel's theorem, T' will itself contain true but unprovable propositions and thus be incomplete. We say that a sufficiently rich, objectively specifiable theory is *essentially incomplete* because not only that theory but all of its objectively specifiable, consistent extensions are incomplete.

On the other hand if we complete T to T' by adding *all possible* true propositions of L as axioms, then T' will no longer be objectively specifiable: its axioms *cannot* be explicitly designated. In other words, we can only conceive of this complete *theory of everything* T' subjectively. It may *exist* objectively, but it cannot be *specified* objectively.

Let us sum up. Descartes' programme was to generate an exact and universal language—an objectively specifiable theory giving a complete description of reality. Gödel's theorem shows there is a logical incompatibility between comprehensiveness and exactness. If we insist on exactness then we *cannot* have completeness, and if we insist on completeness, then we *cannot* have exactness. But Gödel's theorem is itself totally objective. Thus, by Gödel's theorem, *we know absolutely and objectively that we cannot know everything absolutely and objectively.*

Even more: Gödel's theorem shows that indeterminacy is not the exception but the rule, because the vast majority of interesting axiomatic systems will be both objectively specifiable and sufficiently rich (and this has borne itself out in practice).

Thus, whenever we undertake to articulate our understanding of reality (to ourselves or others) we must constantly choose between linear exactness, on one hand, or nonlinear completeness on the other. We cannot have both. It may be that we can generate an exact description of *any given* part of reality, but never of the whole. Or think of it this way: whenever we succeed in giving an exact description of some part of reality, we do so by appealing implicitly to a nonlinear description of some other part of reality. As John Myhill has expressed it: Gödel's theorem shows that there is no non-metaphorical description of (the whole of) reality.

This result enables us greatly to clarify the relationship between scientific theories. A consistent scientific theory is a linear, exact description of a certain part of reality. Suppose we have two different theories which each give an exact description of a different part of reality. Can we not *paste together* these theories and, gradually develop an exact description of the whole? Gödel's theorem tells us in advance that such a strategy cannot succeed. But what happens if we try? In most historical instances, this strategy has produced an incompatibility between the two theories which prevents their being pasted together into one theory.

Indeed, the central problem of modern physics is the incompatibility between relativity theory, which explains gravity and the large-scale structure of the universe, and quantum mechanics, which describes the other three known forces (electromagnetism, weak nuclear, and strong nuclear) and explains the small-scale structure of the universe. The much-discussed superstring theory is an attempt to reconcile this incompatibility by constructing a broader theory that explains both gravity and quantum mechanics. To succeed, such a theory must make some essential modifications either in quantum theory, relativity theory, or both.

Thus, Gödel's incompleteness results constitute a definitive refutation of classic Cartesianism. Are they not also an equally definitive refutation of reductionism? From a strictly logical point of view, Gödel's incompleteness results do indeed refute the strong reductionist thesis, *everything can be objectified,* although it is very difficult for *ideological reductionists* to admit defeat, because victory seems to have been stolen from them at the precise moment they appeared to be on the verge of success. However, one can still consistently maintain reductionism in the weaker form: *everything truly significant can be objectified.* Indeed, there are several strategies for *minimizing* the impact of Gödel's incompleteness results.

Gödel's theorem tells us there will always be deductively undecidable propositions no matter how comprehensive a given, consistent and objectively specifiable, axiomatic theory may be. However, this in itself does not mean necessarily that truly significant or important propositions will in fact be undecidable by a given theory. Furthermore, even if significant uncertainties are detected (as in the case of Heisenberg indeterminacy), they can be dealt with on an *ad hoc* basis by trying to construct a more adequate theory. The new theory will also have undecidable propositions, but not the *same* undecidables as in the previous theory.

In other words, Gödel's results do not have any significant effect on the way science is actually pursued. It is still reasonable to suppose that science may witness an unending succession of ever more comprehensive theories—yet another example of the convergence of an infinite regress. Of course, Gödel's theorem definitely tells us that we will never

have one single absolutely comprehensive theory, but it does not exclude the possibility of a progressive refinement and extension of our
theories. The reductionist can therefore choose to believe that any significant aspect of human experience will, sooner or later, be successfully
objectified.

It is most important to realize that one does not have to be a
reductionist to think objectification by the axiomatic method valid and
useful. Such, in fact, is the philosophical stance of *minimalisim,* which
holds that it is useful to objectify whatever can be objectified. Minimalism
is a strictly positive, non-exclusive stance. It is *downward closed,* holding
that a certain minimum of objectification is necessary for philosophical
cogency, but *upward open,* recognizing that a significant portion of reality, and thus of our inner model, is nonlinear and transrational.

In contrast to minimalism, reductionism is both downward and
upward closed. It disdains whatever lies beyond the objective and the
rational. Reductionisms of any kind are exclusivist by nature. Indeed,
any positive philosophy, "- - -", can be turned into a reductionism simply by adding the global exclusivist clause "and nothing else but - - -."
Thus, a reductionist accepts the minimalist affirmation that
objectification is valid and useful, but adds the exclusivist restriction
that nothing else but objectification is valid and useful.

Reductionism is thus ideological, because it deliberately goes beyond present experience in a negative way, discounting the possibility
that our methods may harbor unforeseen limitations. In contrast,
minimalism is nonideological and pragmatic. It affirms the validity of
what has been achieved in the way of objectification, but remains open
to the possibility both of unforeseen success and of unanticipated limitations. Minimalism is thus *forward compatible* with all future
contingencies, whereas reductionism is awfully liable to find itself either
defending clearly absurd claims, or else beating a humiliating retreat.

Postmodernistic subjectivism—the other extreme response to the
problem of objectification—is, like reductionism, ideological in nature.
Postmodernism holds that objectification is just a solipsistic exercise in
trivialization, a *word-game* having no genuine connection with reality.
This position is based on a strong doctrine of logical apriorism, which
goes far beyond Kant, and which claims (contrary to our analysis above)
that logic has no empirical ground.

Postmodernism is a counter-ideology to reductionism, and is usually articulated in opposition to reductionism, but without any consideration of the pragmatic stance of minimalism. Postmodernists have all heard of Gödel's theorem, though it is most difficult to ascertain how many of them actually understand it. Indeed, Gödel has a kind of cult status among postmodernists, who attempt to apply to Gödel's results the gratuitous *some to all* leap of relativists: since Gödel's theorem shows that total objectification is impossible, then we conclude that no (significant) objectification is possible.[37]

But how can we refute the postmodernist attack on objectification? How can we demonstrate conclusively that objectification is and can be useful and nontrivial?

The practical refutation of the subjectivist attack on scientific verification was the concrete, observable success of such theories as relativity (gravitation) and quantum mechanics. If someone holds that significant objective knowledge of reality is impossible, or that science is just one among a number of equally subjective cultural myths, then let that person explain why scientific theories actually work as well and as consistently as they do.

The practical refutation to the existentialist attack on intersubjective communication was the complexity of modern society. Anyone who claims that no significant intersubjective communication occurs must explain how a complex society such as our own actually works as well as it does (whatever its defects in other regards).

The practical refutation to the postmodernist attack on objectification is the electronic digital computer. Both computer hardware and computer implementation (software) are based on the logic of relations, including the total formalization of large parts of arithmetic, and the use of strictly linear, formalized languages of many kinds and varieties. Let us recall that the computer, unlike the human brain, is not a naturally occurring phenomenon. It had to be conceived, constructed, and implemented. If formal logic and axiomatic systems are simply word games, having no genuine connection with empirical reality, then why do computers work? How is it that we can precalculate the trajectory of an artificial satellite and then execute that trajectory empirically?

Let us recall also that, for most of history, the kinds of intellectual tasks that computers now accomplish were reserved for an elite handful of individuals who were considered to be intellectuals of the highest order, deserving of the respect of the masses. Champion chess players were regarded as supermortals with a unique, superior intellectual gift. And now, a computer has outplayed the current world champion who, in the opinion of many, is the strongest world champion in the history of the game.

These observations are not computer worship. They are facts that must be taken seriously. They show beyond any reasonable doubt that truly significant aspects of our inner model can be successfully objectified.[38] Indeed, had it not been for the stunning success of computer formalization and objectification, the philosophy of reductionism would never have been taken seriously by so many people. All of us who have worked in this area have been surprised by the degree of success we have obtained in objectifying large tracts of human thought that appeared initially to be hopelessly complex and subjective.

Thus, postmodern subjectivism flies in the face of reality itself. We don't really need philosophy to refute it. Yet, the philosophical refutation of various postmodernist doctrines is a useful exercise, which, as we have already experienced in the foregoing, can lead to the clarification of important points and to the relief of sometimes subtle confusions (e.g., the confusion between truth and verification).

3. THE LOGIC OF THE SCIENTIFIC METHOD

Minimalism is a philosophy which holds that there is a positive value in pursuing objectification, without holding that everything can or should be objectified. Science is the enterprise that develops methods and techniques for both objectification and verification. Deductive logic is one of these tools, but it is only one-half of the logic necessary for successful science. The other half is *inductive logic*.

The essential feature of deductive logic is the existence of a complete set of rules for the logic of predicates: to say that Q follows from P by deduction is equivalent to saying that P implies Q, symbolically, $P \vdash Q$ if and only if $P \rightarrow Q$. These rules exist *only* because deduction is a movement from general to particular.

The rule of *Modus Ponens* is an example: if we know that P holds and also that $P \rightarrow Q$, then in particular we know that Q holds. But we cannot reverse this rule. Just to know that Q holds does not usually give us enough information to conclude either that P holds or that P⇒Q.

Another typical rule of predicate logic is the rule of *Universal Specification:* from [For all x,P(x)] to infer P(x). Symbolizing the universal quantifier *for all* by ∀, we can schematize this rule as follows:

$$\frac{\forall x P(x)}{P(x)}$$

The Universal Specification rule simply encodes the obvious fact that whatever is true of all things is true of any particular thing: *every* implies *any.* This, again, is clearly an inference from general to particular.

Inductive logic is a movement from particular to general. It aims at finding a general law which is logically compatible with the given set of particulars and *from which* the set of particulars can be deduced by the rules of predicate logic. For example, an inductive logical principle would have, as its aim, to tell us under what conditions it is legitimate to infer from the particular truths, $P(x_1)$, $P(x_2)$, ..., $P(x_n)$, ... the general affirmation $\forall x P(x)$ (from which each of the $P(x_i)$ can be deduced by a single application of the rule of Univeral Specification). In other words, how much particular truth does it take to make a general truth from which the particulars can be deduced?

One case where it is obviously legitimate to make such an inductive inference is if we have independently verified every logically possible particular instance. However, it is in general very rare that we can do that, and we can never do it if there is an infinite number (or an extremely large finite number) of particular instances to verify. Moreover, even when we can execute such a verification, we can legitimately conclude that the given general case is true, but we still do not have a *rule* for getting the general from the particular.

One successful inductive rule is *mathematical induction:* if P is a property which holds only for natural numbers, 0, 1, 2, etc., and if we can prove (deductively) that P(0) holds and that P(n + 1) holds whenever P(n) holds (i.e., that P(n)⇒P(n + l), for all n), then we can legitimately conclude that ∀xP(x) holds. This rule can be proved (deductively) from the fundamental axioms of the system of natural numbers, first fully presented by Richard Dedekind in 1888.[39] However, viewed as a rule of inference, mathematical induction holds only for a certain limited class of properties and does not, therefore, constitute a general rule of inductive inference analogous to the rules of deductive logic.

The famed British philosopher, John Stuart Mill, formulated four principles of inductive reasoning which he called the methods of difference, of agreement, of residues, and of concomitant variation. It was hoped for a while that appropriate generalizations of *Mill's methods* would lead to a set of rules for inductive logic. However, in the final analysis it turns out that one of the consequences of Gödel's incompleteness theorem definitively excludes the existence of a complete set of rules for inductive inference. Let us take a closer look at this.

Imagine that we are trying to elaborate a scientific theory according to the usual paradigm of scientific method. We begin with a certain number of facts or observation statements. We then seek to explain these facts. What we seek is a theory whose axioms are general propositions from which we can deduce all of the known observation statements. Thus, we are seeking a theory in which each of the observation statements is a theorem.[40]

Of course, the body of facts already constitutes a theory with itself as axioms (and, therefore, as theorems). But we do not usually consider a fact-theory to be a satisfactory explanation of itself. Nor would we consider just any arbitrary extension of the fact-theory as a satisfactory explanation for the observation statements. Of course, an explanation for the fact-theory is certainly an extension of the fact-theory, but it is one in which certain particular deductive (implicational) relationships have been shown to exist (or not to exist).

First of all, the extended theory must be consistent. This means we cannot deduce a contradiction from it. Moreover, we require that we can deduce all of the observation statements from a finite set of general principles (propositions) within the extended theory. The conjunction of these general principles would then be the inductive consequence (generalization) of the original body of facts.[41]

However, we may legitimately consider any consistent extension of the fact-theory as a *possible explanation* for the fact-theory. We evaluate the explanatory power of a possible explanation by exploring deductive relationships within the extended theory.

When accumulating facts, we ask the question *what* (what are things like?). When seeking an explanation, we ask the question *why* (why are things like they are?). Since there are only a finite number of humans, and every human observer can only make a finite number of observations in a finite time, the number of facts is always finite. However, the number of different (logically incompatible) possible explanations for the body of facts is infinite, as follows from Gödel's incompleteness theorem.[42]

This establishes conclusively that rules of inductive logic cannot exist, even in principle, because a finite set of facts does not determine a unique generalization of these facts. As Quine has put it, theory is underdetermined by fact.[43] Nor can we overcome this limitation simply by multiplying the number of observation statements. As long as the body of facts is finite, there will be an infinity of logically different, consistent ways of generalizing from these facts.

To sum up: there exist absolute rules for deductive logic, because deductive logic is a movement from general to particular. There do not exist any such rules for inductive logic, primarily because inductive logic moves from particular to general. Thus, whereas a deductive consequence follows absolutely and objectively from its antecedent, an inductive consequence is only relatively justified and thus always potentially open to question.

Nevertheless, the situation is not quite as bad as it may seem. We have only excluded the possibility of absolute rules for inductive logic, comparable to the absolute rules of deductive logic. However, we have not excluded the existence of *principles* of inductive logic that help guide us to find the most reasonable generalization in the light of current knowledge.

The first, and most basic of these principles is the *validity principle,* which states that our generalized theory must not only be consistent but also logically compatible with all observations. With regard to validity, we find ourselves in an almost humorous situation. It is possible to prove absolutely that a theory is invalid, because if some of the theory's deductive consequences (which we call its *predictions*) flagrantly contradict highly authenticated observations, then the theory cannot be valid. The theory will have to be abandoned or else modified in some way. But no matter how many predictions of the theory have been confirmed by observation, the possibility always remains of the theory's future invalidation as a result either of novel predictions that contradict known evidence or novel evidence that contradicts known predictions.

Another principle is *conservativity*. Our example above of the process of elaborating a scientific theory, starting with a certain number of observation statements, was presented in abstraction from any context. Clearly, if our only method of finding an inductive generalization from a fact-theory was to consider each of the infinity of possible explanations one by one in arbitrary sequence, scientific advances would be impossible save by absolute miracle. However, in the reality of scientific practice, we are always elaborating a new theory not only with respect to the relevant facts, but also with respect to a pre-existing *background theory*—a theory which will already have proved itself in many respects. This background theory usually renders certain generalizations of the fact-theory considerably more reasonable than others.

For example, suppose we are trying to modify the background theory to accommodate new facts. One technique is to look for a theory that accommodates the new facts while minimizing changes to the background theory. This conservative approach to theory modification eliminates those possible explanations for the new facts which make gratuitous or arbitrary changes to the background theory, and, at the same time, suggests positive ways of building the new theory. Thus, conservativity with respect to the background theory is one of the guiding principles of inductive logic.[44]

Yet another principle is *Occam's razor*, otherwise known as the principle of parsimony or simplicity. This principle addresses the issue of the introduction of new nonobservables as explanations for the new fact-theory. The simplicity principle says that we should introduce only those abstract notions that appear irreducibly necessary to explain observation.

A good example of an application of the simplicity principle is the original Newtonian theory of gravity. The force of gravity is, itself, an unobservable force. What we observe is a persistent deviation from randomness in the behavior of free objects in the presence of a large mass like the earth. Nothing that we can observe physically constrains the objects to move downward, but they all do. The minimally simple explanation is that there is some nonobservable force that makes them go down. Once we posit this force and observe that the acceleration it causes is the same for all bodies, we immediately have Newton's theory.

Another principle is *adequacy*. The new theory must really explain all of the fact-theory, not just part of it. Indeed, if we are fortunate, the new theory may be superadequate: it may explain much more than just the original fact theory. (Again, Newton's theory of gravity, which explained planetary motion as well as falling objects, is an example.)

There is a certain trade-off between simplicity and adequacy. We might be willing to accept a more lavish or complicated theory if it is substantially more adequate than a simpler one. Again, these are qualitative principles, not absolute rules, and the effective use of inductive logic involves openness to future reevaluation of inductive inferences in the light of new information.[45]

Besides these general methodological principles, modern science has generated certain substantive principles which eliminate the need for explanations in some cases. One of these is the second law of thermodynamics or the law of entropy. This law says that order, or the evolution of a system towards order, is improbable, and that disorder, or the degeneration towards disorder, is a probable (natural) configuration. In the light of this law, many fact-theories do not necessitate an explanation. If our observations of a system show a steady increase in disorder, then we do not have to bother looking for a cause to this phenomenon: this is the natural state of affairs. But if we observe a system that is evolving persistently towards increased order, then there *must* be some cause (whether observable or not) for the phenomenon, and we must seek out that cause.

More generally, we can often introduce a *probability measure* of the likelihood of a given theory being true relative to another theory. We may say that a given theory has *higher probability* of truth than another. Such a measure is always relative to the current state of our knowledge. New information can radically change these probability measures, making a previously discarded theory now the favored one.

Rather than trying to keep constantly in mind each of these principles and parameters of inductive inference, philosophers of science have more recently formulated a *lumped parameter* principle of *plausible inference,* which we can formulate as follows: to infer, from a given fact-theory, to the best possible (epistemologically optimal) explanation in the light of current knowledge. Here *best possible* is meant to include consideration of validity, conservativity, simplicity, adequacy, and probability (if relevant).

If we extend the notion of plausible inference to include deduction as well as induction (the absolutely certain is *a fortiori* plausible), then we can say that the basic logic of science is plausible reasoning. When rules of deduction are applicable we use them. Otherwise, we resort to the best possible explanation in the light of current knowledge. It is by an alternation of deduction and induction—of particularization and of generalization starting with observation—that science is built up.

It may seem at first that the logic of plausibility would be too weak to account for the success of science, but such a view ignores how easy it is for our emotional prejudices to insinuate themselves into even the most rigorous attempts at theory construction. We all feel that we reason plausibly most of the time, but the fact is that we don't. It is only by a strong will to rationality that we can consistently apply the plausibility principle without lapsing into unwarranted (implausible) inferences.[46]

We have begun our discussion of inductive inference by stressing the fact that there exists an infinity of possible explanations consistent with any given finite set of facts. But in practice, we can only consider a theory once it has been conceived in the first place. Thus, in practice our choice is not among all the infinity of possible explanations, but only among the possible explanations that we actually know. It is a highly creative task to conceive of even one possible explanation for a given fact-theory. There is, in short, a fundamental methodological discontinuity between fact-gathering and theory-conception. We can go on gathering new facts forever, but until someone has the creativity to conceive of a possible explanation for these facts, we have no theory to test for plausibility.

Thus, the common notion that science is determined by hard fact alone, in presumed contrast to the speculative nature of philosophy or religion, is simply false. Science involves an essential and irreducible element of creative theorizing. Nevertheless, no matter how creative a conceived theory may be, unless it passes the tests of validity, simplicity, and adequacy, it will not be accepted as justified by the logic of plausibility.

V. MINIMALISTIC METAPHYSICS

1. PLAUSIBLE LOGIC AS PHILOSOPHICAL METHOD

In the preceeding sections, we have dealt primarily with certain methodological issues related to science and philosophy. We have put forward as a normative methodological ideal a certain philosophy of minimalism, which holds that it is useful and legitimate to pursue objectification, but which renounces the reductionistic notion that everything can or should be objectified.

In certain contexts—when dealing with computer languages, for example—the practical difference between reductionism and minimalism is quite small, because the residue of subjectivity that separates them is almost negligible. However, the more comprehensive the subject matter, the greater the practical difference between minimalism and reductionism. In particular, when we arrive at philosophy, reductionism has become a full-scale, dogmatically-held philosophical ideology which asserts that everything worthwhile can be objectified. There is an immense gap between such an ideology and the counter-ideology of subjectivism and postmodernism, which hold that objectification is simply a word game and that nothing really worthwhile can be objectified.

Because many philosophers tend to fall into one of these two camps, the approach of non-dogmatic, empirically-grounded minimalism has never been systematically applied to substantive philosophical issues. Thus, not only as an example or exercise but also as an intrinsically valuable enterprise, we propose to deal with some classical philosophical problems and issues within the minimalistic framework. We will begin with some assumptions and definitions, which we will state with a somewhat greater degree of formality than has been the case in the foregoing text.

2. EXISTENCE

First, and most basic, is the assumption there is something and not nothing. This assumption is logically prior even to solipsism, which supposed that there is only subjective existence. One might be tempted to assert, more boldly, that we certainly know that something exists, because if, literally, nothing existed then we would not be here to ask the question as to whether anything existed. Even if our perception of the world and of ourselves is an illusion, still something (the illusory self contemplating an illusory reality) exists.

This reasoning (which goes back to Descartes) is certainly correct, however, it is part of the method of minimalism that we make every assumption explicit, regardless of how obvious or reasonable it may be. This is because we are now equally interested both in the results of our process (the conclusions we draw) and the process itself (the method by which we arrive at our conclusions).

We now define *reality* as the totality of (actual) existence, past, present, and future. Reality is everything there *is,* where the verb *to be* is used in an atemporal or eternal sense. This is a minimalist definition of reality, because it puts the least possible presuppositions on the nature of reality. For example, it allows for the existence of transtemporal entities (entities existing outside of space-time) without actively supposing that such entities do in fact exist. Thus, time is regarded as an independent dimension, and time-bound entities are time-parametered (existing in the past, present, or future).[47]

Reality, as we have defined it, is comprised of actual existence and does not include such things as potential or possible existences (except insofar as these terms are taken as metaphors for actually existing configurations which allow for certain other actually existing configurations in the future).

Next, we define a *phenomenon* as some (nonempty) portion of reality. Thus, every existent is a phenomenon, and reality itself is just one big phenomenon. Reality and existence are thus interdefinable. Reality is the sum of all existence and an existent is some (nonempty) part of reality.

It is most important to see that these definitions are completely objective, and do not depend for their meaning on any assumptions concerning the extent of human knowledge. For example, we do not suppose that we can have an adequate conception of reality, or that we can know, even in principle, everything there is. Nor do we suppose that we can, in any given case, determine the exact boundaries of a given phenomenon. But what is beyond dispute is that, whenever we consider anything short of the whole of reality, we are considering a phenomenon that is limited in some way. In this context, *limited* does not mean isolated or unconnected with other phenomena.[48]

The same primary logic that justifies the assumption that something exists (see note 47) also justifies the assumption that human consciousness exists. Indeed, the very fact that we are conscious of posing the question of consciousness is primary, irreducible evidence that consciousness exists. Our (individual) consciousness creates a private world of inner states (phenomena) to which only we have direct, unmediated, and privileged access. This world of inner phenomena constitutes our *subjectivity*. Thus, an individual's subjectivity is comprised precisely of all those phenomena to which only that individual has direct, unmediated access.

We say that a phenomenon is *subjective* if it is wholly internal to one or more human subjects. The sum total of all subjective phenomena constitutes *subjective reality*. By *objective reality* we mean everything outside of subjective reality (objective reality is thus the Boolean complement of subjective reality). An objective phenomenon is a phenomenon that is wholly external to human subjectivity.

Again, these definitions are perfectly objective. They do not suppose that we can always know whether a given phenomenon is objective or subjective. The definition itself does not even presuppose that there is an objective reality. It only gives a defining characteristic of objectivity (i.e., the criterion something must satisfy in order to count as objective).

Of course, we have already given, in the early sections of this monograph, strong arguments against solipsism and other extreme forms of subjectivism. But the important point to see here is that the present definitions are logically prior to these philosophical questions. Nor do these definitions depend for their cogency on one or another solution to these problems.

Another category of reality is constituted by those phenomena which can be observed or sensed by all normally endowed human subjects. We designate this category as *concrete reality*. A concrete phenomenon is one to which all normally endowed human subjects have equal, unprivileged, and direct access, an access unmediated by any subjectivity other than that of the individual subject himself/herself. Since any individual subject has privileged and direct access to his or her internal states, there will always be at least one human subject who has privileged access to some part of any given subjective phenomenon. Hence, no concrete phenomenon can be subjective: concrete reality is wholly contained within objective reality.

Of course, this equality of access to concrete objects is an equality-in-principle. For example, if I am closer to an object than you are, then I have, momentarily, greater access to it than do you. But the equality-in-principle means that you and I can change places and thus you can have the same access I now have. The access of each individual to concrete objects is of course mediated to him through the agency of his own subjectivity via the inner sensations and states provoked within him by his encounter with the concrete object. But the important point is that the individual does not depend on the experience or protocol of other subjects in order to observe a concrete object. The only subjectivity he must rely upon is his own.

The complement to concrete reality is *abstract* reality. Abstract reality thus includes all of subjective reality and also that portion of objective reality to which we have no direct access whatever. We designate the latter category as *invisible* or *nonobservable* reality. Invisible reality is constituted by such forces and entities as gravity or the individual photons of light. The existence of such forces and entities can only be detected indirectly, by the effect these invisible phenomena have on observable reality. For example, we observe the downward falling of unsupported concrete objects, but we do not observe the force of gravity that makes such objects fall. The objective reality of this force is deduced from the fact that unsupported objects do not behave randomly in the presence of a large mass such as the earth, but rather all move in a downward direction.

Again, let us stress that our definition of concreteness in no wise depends upon our being able, practically, to draw a clear boundary between the observable and the nonobservable. Extremely small or extremely distant objects may be presently unobservable but become observable in the future through the acquisition of more refined techniques of observation. This means that these objects were always observable in principle and thus concrete, even though the boundary between the practically observable and unobservable may change. But this does not undermine the objectivity of the definition itself, because the definition only requires that there be a boundary, not that we can determine the boundary in every case.

From now on, when we speak of a phenomenon A as, say, subjective or concrete, we will mean that A is wholly contained within the named category. It is quite possible and may frequently occur, that a phenomenon cuts across several categories, e.g., it may have both a concrete and an abstract dimension, or both a subjective and an objective aspect.

Notice that all these categories tell us nothing about the actual structure of objective reality. They only tell us something about the relationship between our subjectivity and reality. Notice in particular that we have not attempted to define material or physical reality as opposed to spiritual or non-material reality. In fact, we will never have need of such notions. In our scheme, the crucial division within objective reality is between observable and nonobservable. Moreover, it is an essential feature of the method of minimalism that we will never assume anything about nonobservable reality beyond what can be plausibly inferred from our observations of concrete reality. We say that our metaphysics is thus *empirically grounded.*[49]

However, we have gone about as far as we can go with our agnosticism about the structure of objective reality. We must now make some more explicitly metaphysical definitions and assumptions concerning reality.

3. PART AND WHOLE: COMPOSITION AND THE COMPONENTHOOD RELATION

We now assume that any existent phenomenon must be either simple or composite. That is, a phenomenon B may be composed of other phenomena A, $A \neq B$, or else B may have no components at all, in which case it is a simple (unified) indivisible whole. We symbolize the componenthood relationship by a stylized epsilon symbol $\in$. Thus, $A \in B$ means "The phenomenon A is a component of the phenomenon B." Thus, to say that B is *composite* is to say that $A \in B$ holds for at least one phenomenon A (B has at least one component, namely A). If, for a given B, $A \in B$ holds for no A whatsoever, then B is *simple* or *noncomposite*.

According to modern physical theory, all macrophysical, concrete objects are composites, for they are composed, for example, of electrons, protons, and neutrons. The only candidates for simplicity are the elementary particles of quantum theory. The question of whether the currently known elementary particles are in fact noncomposite is still an open question in modern physics.

Notice that a component A of B need not be an immediate component of B. It is logically possible that $A \in A_1 \in A_2 \in A_3 \in \ldots A_n \in B$, where A itself and each of the A_i are all different components of B. We say that A is an *immediate component* of B if $A \in B$ and if there is no phenomenon D such that $A \in D \in B$. By an *ultimate* component of B we mean some component $A \in B$ such that no component $E \in A$ is a component of B. (Thus, any simple component of B is an ultimate component, but in general an ultimate component need not be simple.)

By definition, a phenomenon B is composite if it has components. If B is itself a component of some other phenomenon A, then we say that B is an *entity*. We assume that all simple phenomena are entities. Composite phenomena in general are also called *systems*. Thus, some systems are entities and some are not.

Let us now sum up our ontological categories. With respect to composition, we have a hierarchy of complexity. At the lowest level are the simple entities. A simple entity A is a component but does not have any components: $? \notin A \in B$, for some B. Next are the entity-systems A which both have components and are components: $E \in A \in B$, for some E and B. Finally, there are the composite phenomena (systems) A which have components B, but never are themselves components: $B \in A \notin ?$.

We can often observe and manipulate the composite nature of macrophysical objects: we can take them apart and sometimes put them back together. Thus, the metaphysical notion of composition is thoroughly grounded empirically. This does not mean that we have a clear understanding of what composition or simplicity mean in all contexts. For example, is a subjective idea simple or composite? On the one hand, the notion of *half an idea* doesn't make much sense. On the other hand, it is not unreasonable to suppose that there may be a certain number of fundamental, simple ideas which form the components of more complex, composite ideas. Again, the point is that we do not have to resolve such issues in order for the metaphysical notion of composition to be objective and empirically grounded. What we do assume, of course, is that the question as to whether ideas are simple or composite is a meaningful question. We assumed this when we supposed that every existing phenomenon is either composite or simple.

We now use the componenthood relationship ∈ to define another useful relationship, the containment relation ⊂, which is defined only between systems. We say that a system A is a *subsystem* of a system B, and we write A⊂B, if every component E∈A is also a component E∈B. In this case, we also say that A is *contained in* B or that A is a *portion* of B.

Initially it may seem difficult to grasp the difference between componenthood and containment. The first step is to realize that componenthood is the more general and more fundamental notion, because noncomposites can be components but never subsystems (since they are not systems). Secondly, a subsystem can be both a component and a subsystem of another system; one does not necessarily exclude the other.[50]

Let us give a few examples. Consider the human body as a biological system. The immediate components of the body are its biological subsystems and the immediate components of these biological subsystems are the organs that comprise them.[51] Thus, the digestive system is both a component of the body and also a subsystem of the body. The immediate components of the digestive sytems are organs such as the stomach or the small intestine. The ultimate organic components of the body as an organism are its cells. The ultimate components of the body viewed as a physical object are the elementary particles (e.g., electrons or protons) which are components of the atoms that occur in the various cells of the body. All of the components, except possibly some of the ultimate components, are also systems. But an ultimate component cannot be a subsystem (by definition, see above).

Or, consider a leaved tree. An individual leaf is a component of the tree and the set of all leaves is a subsystem, but not a component of the tree.[52]

The following simple geometrical example should be helpful in understanding the difference between components and subsystems. Let B be the system whose components are precisely the points inside the larger circle. A is the system whose components are the points within the smaller circle. Since the perimeter of A is wholly within the perimeter of B, every point E in A is also a point in B. So by definition, A is a subsystem (portion) of B. But A is not a component of B because only points are components, and A is not a point but rather a set of points. Thus, every point E in A is a component of both A and B, but is a subsystem of neither (because the points are the ultimate components of the systems A and B).

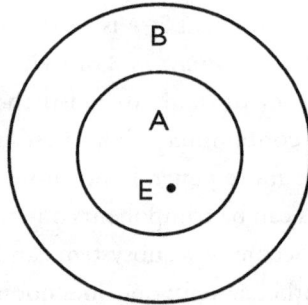

We can also use these notions of componenthood and containment to make more precise our original definitions of reality and phenomena. Let us use the symbol V to stand for the whole of reality. Since by definition every composite phenomenon B is a portion of V, every such B is contained in V, B⊂V. Thus, by definition every component E∈B is a component of V, E∈V. But components of systems are precisely what we have defined as entities. Thus, every entity is a component of V. Conversely, a component of V, E∈V, is an entity by definition (it is a component of something, namely V). In sum: *to be an entity is to be a component of* V. Thus reality, V, is that phenomenon whose components are precisely all existent entitites. Moreover, composite entities are both components and subsystems of V. Systems that are not entities are subsystems of V, but not components of V.

Let us say that a phenomenon A is a *part* of a phenomenon B if A is either a component or a subsystem of B. With this terminology, we can say that every existing phenomenon B is a part of reality V: either B∈V or B⊂V. We can also reformulate, as a formal principle, our assumption that something exists:

P.0. V is composite.

4. CAUSALITY

We now consider a second relationship that may exist between phenomena: the causality relation. Let A and B be two phenomena (composite or not). We say that A *causes* B, and we write A→B, if it is the case that B exists by virtue of A. If, for some A and B, A→B holds, then A is a *cause* of B and B an *effect* (or *result*) of A. If there is some A≠B such that A→B, then we say that B is *caused* or *other-caused*. If B→B, then we say that B is *uncaused* or *self-caused*. Finally, if for no A whatsoever do we have A→B, then we say that B is *without a cause*.

The fundamental principle of the causality relationship, and the first non-trivial principle of our metaphysics is the *principle of sufficient reason*. It says essentially that no phenomenon can exist without a cause. The precise formulation is as follows:

P.1. Every existent phenomenon B is either caused (other-caused) or uncaused (self-caused), and never both.

Before we discuss the philosophical cogency of this principle, let us be sure we understand what it says. In the first place, it does not directly posit the existence of anything. It does not say that there are uncaused phenomena (or caused phenomena). But it does say that there are no phenomena that exist without a cause (i.e., that have no causal link either with some other phenomenon or with themselves (self-causation)). Moreover, it says that the categories of self-causation and other-causation are mutually exclusive: a phenomenon cannot be both self-caused and other-caused. So, for example, if we have determined that a certain B is self-caused (i.e., B→B), then by that fact (and P.1), B cannot be other-caused (i.e., A→B holds only when A=B). Conversely, if we have determined that A→B holds for some A≠B, then B→B cannot hold.

The principle of sufficient reason means that nothing can exist without a reason for its existence. This reason must be either within itself (self-causation) or else the reason must lie in some other existent (other-causation). The case B→B is thus a state of *self-sufficiency;* the phenomenon B contains within itself the reason for itself. It exists by virtue of itself alone. This is why caused and uncaused are mutually exclusive categories: a phenomenon cannot be self-sufficient and, at the same time, owe its existence to something other than itself. It cannot exist by virtue of itself and also by virtue of something other than itself. Think of causation as a dependency relationship. A phenomenon cannot both depend on itself alone and also depend on something other than itself.

Is causality empirically grounded? The philosopher Hume argued that it is not, and certainly our definition of A→B (B exists by virtue of A) is not empirical but thoroughly metaphysical. However, Hume's arguments only establish that causal links between observable phenomena are logically inferred from empirical observation rather than observed directly. This point is now well-understood in science, and does not undermine the cogency of the notion of causation itself.

In this regard, let us consider once again our well-worn example of gravity. We observe the fact that unsupported objects fall to the ground, but we do not observe the force of gravity itself—the causal link between the initial position of the free object and its final position at rest on the ground. An unsupported object is free to move in all directions, but it always moves downward. What we observe, then, is a persistent deviation from randomness, without any observable cause for this deviation. In such cases, the scientific logic of plausible inference allows us (indeed, compels us) to infer that there is some nonobservable force that causes the observed behavior. All of the fundamental forces of physics have been discovered by this indirect reasoning, and none of these forces is directly observable in itself.

Thus, we accept as a fundamental feature of causality that causal links (relationships) are inferred, not observed. But there is nonetheless an empirical basis for such inference. If indeed A→B holds—if B exists by virtue of A—then there cannot ever be a case of A without B. This gives us at least a partial (negative) empirical test for causality. If ever we observe an instance of A without B, then there cannot be a causal link from A to B. However, no matter how many times we observe A followed by B, we can never conclude absolutely—from these observations alone—that A→B holds. (See also the discussion above of inductive inference in science.)

Thus, "never A without B" is a minimal empirically necessary indication that B exists by virtue of A. The former condition is thus an empirical ground for the latter. By respecting this minimal empirical condition—by refusing to infer a causal link in its absence—we are assured that we can never have an empirical counterexample to our metaphysical causality relationship. We may, of course, presume such a causal link in error, but we are always committed to revising that presumption as soon as the necessary contrary evidence is forthcoming.[53]

5. CAUSALITY AND REASON

It is often debated whether the universe is *rational* or can be *rationally understood.* We have already seen in our previous discussion that *reason* refers to a certain internal process of the human mind (making our assumptions explicit). Thus, strictly speaking it is we humans who are either rational or irrational, not reality itself. However, the causality relationship, and principle P.1 in particular, enable us to give a coherent meaning to the notion of the rationality of reality.

Our life can be viewed as a sequence of interactions or encounters with reality. In each such encounter, we confront some particular aspect of reality—some phenomenon B. Our senses give us information about the concrete aspect of B and its structure. This is descriptive information that essentially answers the question *how?* (how in fact is B structured—what are its qualities and attributes?). As our minds begin to process this information, there arises another category of questions— the *why?* questions. We are not satisfied just to recognize that B *is* a certain way. We want to understand what *makes* B the way it is. We are looking for a cause A of B, and the principle P.1 tells us that this question *always has* an answer (whether we can find it or not).

A cause A of a phenomenon B is the counterpart in objective reality of an assumption A′ from which we can logically deduce a certain conclusion B′. Thus, P.1 is the precondition of rationality. This principle says that reason—the subjective process of making our assumptions about reality explicit—has the potential or the capacity to give us true information (truth) about the structure of reality.

In other words, when our empirical observations of a phenomenon B are accurate, we can formulate a proposition B′ which is a true and accurate (though not complete) description of B. If, further, A causes B, then the propositon A′ will logically imply the proposition B′. In this way, the logical relationship of implication (or deduction) mirrors or reflects the objective relationship of causality: $A′ \Rightarrow B′$ if and only if $A \rightarrow B$ holds.

The following diagram gives a fuller representation of the relationship between deduction and causality. In this particular example, we assume that the phenomena A and B are totally objective, but that assumption is not essential since the causality relationship is universal (i.e., it holds for all categories of reality).

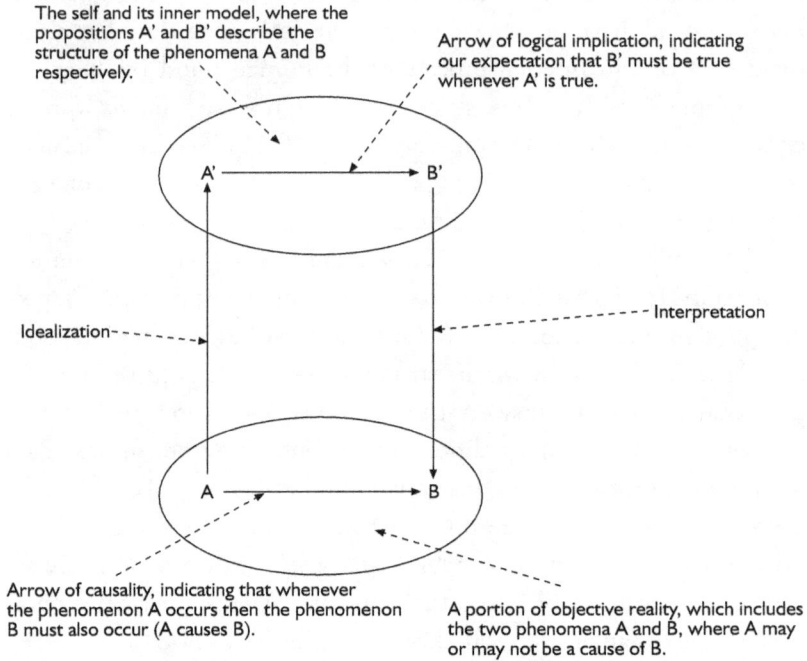

The self and its inner model, where the propositions A' and B' describe the structure of the phenomena A and B respectively.

Arrow of logical implication, indicating our expectation that B' must be true whenever A' is true.

Interpretation

Idealization

Arrow of causality, indicating that whenever the phenomenon A occurs then the phenomenon B must also occur (A causes B).

A portion of objective reality, which includes the two phenomena A and B, where A may or may not be a cause of B.

Relationship Between the Inner Model and Reality

By the mental process of idealization, we represent within our subjectivity (mind) the two observed (or conceived) phenomena A and B, by two propositions A' and B' each of which describes the corresponding phenomenon as existing in the way we have perceived or conceived it. Our inner model will be correct if our idealization process has correctly identified and represented (reflected) the fundamental logical features of the phenomena A and B. If our model is in fact correct and if the phenomenon A does in fact cause the phenomenon B, then our proposition A' will logically imply B'. But if our formulation of propositions A' and B' is incorrect (our inner model is inaccurate), then A' may imply B' even if A does not cause B, or else A' may not imply B' even though A does in fact cause B. In either of the last two cases, our prediction or expectation, represented by the arrow of interpretation, will not be realized. But, if our inner model is accurate, and if A does in fact cause B, then our expectation (prediction) will be realized, and we can go from A to B either directly (experimentation) or else by the sequence idealization-implication-interpretation (reason).

It should be clear that idealization and interpretation are simply two aspects of the unified process by which our inner model of reality is constructed on the basis of our experience of reality. In the common sense approach to life (see discussion in the foregoing), this ongoing process is largely spontaneous (unconscious). As we become conscious of the process (the transition from common sense to reason), we can see that it involves a continual dialectic between an inward move from reality towards our inner model (idealization) and an outward move from the inner model towards reality (interpretation).

At the beginning of the transition from common sense to reason, we are very reliant on direct experience of reality (trial and error, experimentation). However, as the structure of our inner model becomes increasingly sophisticated, we grow progressively less dependent on direct experience and more confident in our ability to idealize, deduce, and interpret.

Suppose for example that you can count but cannot add. If you put seven apples together with eight other apples, you can count the result and conclude that there are, in fact, fifteen apples. But with the help of the mental operation of addition (which is a form of deduction), you can proceed as follows. First you represent the two sets of apples by the numbers 7 and 8 (idealization). You then add 7 and 8 to obtain the number 15 (deduction). Finally, you interpret the result (the number 15) as representing the actual quantity of apples that will (or would!) result from putting together the two sets.

With the use of reason, you can actually predict the result of a contemplated operation, without actually having to perform the operation. Without reason (in the above example, when you cannot add), you must actually perform the operation physically (putting the apples together) and then experience concretely the results (counting the assembled apples). In other words, reason allows us to replace concrete, physical manipulations of reality by a purely subjective manipulation of abstract mental entities (the numbers in the above example). This example is also a simple illustration of the way that purely abstract mental entities (numbers again) can be used to reflect or represent truths about objective reality (e.g., quantities of apples).

Let us stress again the importance of the fact that causality and composition are binary relations between phenomena and not simply qualities or attributes of phenomena. Until the late 19th century, the only formal logic used by philosophers was Aristotle's syllogistic, which is a logic only of attributes (not relations). Attributional logic is reasonably adequate for the *how* part of our enterprise, but woefully inadequate when it comes to the *why?* question of causality.

Aristotle pointed out that to know some phenomenon B is to know its properties—what attributes are true or false of B. Grass is green, fire burns, water flows. We know things by comparing the attributes they share and the attributes that differentiate them from each other. Total knowledge of a phenomenon B would be to know every property that is true of B (and therefore, by the same token, every property that is not true of B).

But when we begin to ask *why* a phenomenon B has a certain attribute, then the inadequacies of the attributional approach become quickly apparent. Classical metaphysics is therefore full of such *non-answers* as "grass is green because it is the nature of grass to be green; fire burns because that is the nature of fire; water flows because it is inherent in the nature of water to flow." Or, if one has a religious bent, the answer might be that "God *made* grass to be green, fire to burn, and water to flow—that's why."

These (non)answers to the why question amount to a negation of principle P.1, because they affirm that the phenomenon B just is the way it is—without any reason for its being that way. But, in the light of the principle of sufficient reason, we can say that we know in advance that there is some reason (cause) A why B has the properties it has. In other words, causes are explanations for phenomena, and reasoning about causes involves us necessarily in relational logic since causality is a relationship and not just an attribute (though of course *other-causedness* and *self-causedness* are attributes that derive from the causality relationship).

Let us apply P.1 to, say, the greenness of grass. Why indeed is grass green? The answer is composite. One part of the reason has to do with the structure of white light—the fact that the entire spectrum of colors is enfolded within it. The other part relates to attributes of grass itself, whose structure involves a pigmental substance that has the property of absorbing the whole spectrum of light except for the green portion, which it reflects when white light is incident upon it. Note that this is a case of other-causedness, because self-causation means that the entire cause has to be within the phenomenon itself. In this case, the cause is partly within the phenomenon itself (the pigmental substance within grass) but partly outside of the phenomenon (the nature of white light).

Note also that our explanation of the greenness of grass is wholly objective, because we appeal to the definition of colors in terms of wavelengths of light. Thus, our explanation does not involve any such supposed subjectivist philosophical conundrums as to whether grass is still green when there is no one to observe it. Similarly objective explanations can be given for the burning of fire and the flowing of water.

Let us note that all of these objective explanations for concrete phenomena have been generated by modern science. This fact illustrates the above observation that the principle P.1 of sufficient reason is the precondition for rationality (and rationality the basis of science).

6. CAUSALITY AND COMPOSITION

Causality and composition are two different, independent relationships. Neither presupposes the other. Yet, there must be some interaction between these relations. We posit two empirically grounded metaphysical principles which link causality and composition. The first is the *potency principle:*

> *P.2. Suppose that* A→B *holds, where* B *is composite. Then* A→E *also holds where* E *is any part of* B *(i.e., where either* E∈B *or* E⊂B*).*

The logic of P.2 is apparent upon a little reflection. A composite is made up of its parts and thus owes its existence to the existence of its parts. If A→B holds (B exists by virtue of A)—if A is a phenomenon capable in and of itself of producing (all of) B—then in so doing, A must certainly be able to produce every part of B.

We can also formulate this in Aristotlean terms. Everything is made of a substance and has a form (structure). The substance of a composite system consists of the individual components that make it up, while its structure consists of the various relationships between the components. In particular, these relationships are reflected within the various subsystems of the composite. Thus, to produce a composite system involves producing both its components and its proper subsystems (cf. note 50).

However, the converse does not hold: producing all of the components and proper subsystems of B may not be sufficient to produce B.

The notion of causality expressed by the principle P.2 is that of *complete cause* (philosophy recognizes several different notions of *cause*). The common-sense (and scientific) notion of causality corresponds rather to Aristotle's notion of an *efficient* cause. The efficient cause is the straw that finally breaks the camel's back. The complete cause is all of the other straws which, together with the last one, have broken the back of the camel. We can make an equation: $CC=IP+EC$, "The complete cause equals the initial phenomenon plus the efficient cause."

Science concentrates on the efficient cause because a given scientific investigation usually moves carefully from the known towards the unknown. The initial phenomenon is given and generally rather well known, as is the observed effect. What a specific experiment seeks to determine is the precise nature of the efficient cause of the effect (i.e., exactly what has to be added to the initial phenomenon to produce the observed (or desired) effect). Scientists of course know it is not the efficient cause alone that produces the effect, but rather the efficient cause (whatever it turns out to be) plus the initial phenomenon. Since the initial phenomenon and its features are presumed known, scientists speak loosely of the efficient cause, once it is known, as *the* cause, but everyone is aware of the imprecision in this way of speaking.

However, the minimalistic method we are using here does not presume any context and seeks to make everything as explicit as possible. Thus we are led naturally to the notion of complete cause and the principle P.2. There can of course be more than one complete cause for a given effect, but any two such causes are equivalent in the sense that they are each capable, in and of themselves, of producing the effect in question. But no such equivalence obtains for efficient causes since the contexts may be so different.

Suppose for example the effect in question is that a given stone falls from a height of five feet to the earth. If the presumed context is the earth and the free stone at a height of five feet, then the efficient cause is the force of gravitational attraction. However, if the presumed context is the earth, the stone, and the force of gravity between them, then the efficient cause becomes whatever has released the stone at a height of five feet (e.g., my letting it go free). However, the complete cause is the same in both cases.

The success of science in building verifiable theories with robust predictivity provides ample empirical grounding for the notion of efficient cause. The above analysis and examples show that the notion of complete cause is equally grounded empirically. Thus, principle P.2 is empirically grounded.

We now consider one more principle that relates causality and composition, the *limitation principle*:

P.3. $A \rightarrow E$ *cannot hold if* E *is a component of* A, $E \in A$.

Principle P.3 asserts that a composite can never be the cause of one of its own components. Indeed, as we have already seen above in our discussion of substance and form, the existence of a composite whole depends both on its components (its substance) and the various relationships between these components (its form). Thus, the existence of a component cannot be due to the composite of which it is a part, because that composite does not even exist until all its components are formed. It is quite conceivable that the whole comes into existence simultaneously with its components, under the influence of some causal agent, but not that the whole has caused (and therefore pre-existed) one of its proper parts.

The logic of P.3 seems impeccable, but there are some cases which, if not handled thoughtfully, can appear to contradict this principle. For example, cells in my body are continually dying out and being replaced by new cells. Suppose my body manufactures a new white cell in the next instant. Isn't this a case where the whole (my body) has been the cause of one of its own parts (the new white cell)?

The solution to this apparent problem becomes immediately clear when we observe that the new body—the one that contains the new white cell—is not the same as the (old) body which manufactured (and thus caused) the new white cell. We have to remember that any time-parametered phenomenon consists of a succession of *stages* (which are themselves phenomena), a stage being the state of the phenomenon at a given instant of time. Thus, in the above example, we must distinguish between the body B_1 at time t_1 and the body B_2 at time t_2, where we understand that $B_2 = B'_1 + WC$, where B'_1 is B_1 however modified in the process of producing the new white cell WC. The correct causality relation is then $B_1 \rightarrow WC$, which does not contradict P.3, and not the false relation $B_2 \rightarrow WC$.

We also have the option of considering the body as a single dynamical system (process) which occupies a certain portion of space-time. However, now the components of the body are no longer single cells but the processes by which the process-body's cells have been produced during its entire lifetime. In this case, the process-body is more correctly viewed as a result of these process-components than as their cause.

Of course, it is quite correct to say that the process-body and its process-components exist and interact simultaneously. Neither precedes the other, and neither can exist without the other. Such interaction and interdependence between whole and part is the very nature of all dynamical systems. But this does not in itself imply a causal relation between whole and part. For example, in the case of the human body, the cause of the process-body and its process-components is, first of all, the uniting of a male and a female gamete to form the initial zygote, plus the various environmental conditions that make this organism viable (e.g., the mother's womb which provides such things as protection and nutrition). More generally, in accord with the second law of thermodynamics, no dynamical (physical) system could cause/maintain a nondegenerating component process on its own (i.e., without the help of an outside causal agent in the form of energy input into the system).

The above examples are important in establishing that principle P.3 is empirically grounded, but their complexity should not be allowed to obscure the simple and straightforward logic of P.3. By definition, a composite whole exists only when all of its components exist. Thus, it is logically impossible for the existence of a whole to precede (logically or temporally) the existence of its components. At best it can come into existence simultaneously with its components, but this in no wise implies that the whole is the cause of the components.

Notice, however, that P.3 does not exclude the possibility of a component preceeding and causing a whole of which it is part. A simple example is the solar system. According to one viable theory of this system, all of the planets were once a part of the sun and were spun off from the sun. Their rotations around the sun are held to result from an equilibrium between the centripetal force of their expulsion from the original sun, and the gravitational attraction of the sun. Moreover, the structure and nature of each planet is wholly determined by its relationship to the sun (distance, speed of rotation, etc.). Thus, it is the sun and its dynamics that have produced the solar system in its current form, and not the solar sytem as a whole that has produced the sun.

7. GOD AND SUCH

We now have before us four empirically grounded, and therefore plausibly true, metaphysical principles (P.0-P.3). We list them together for easy reference in the ensuing text.

P.0. V *is composite.*

P.1. Every existing phenomenon B *is either caused (other-caused) or uncaused (self-caused),* and never both.

P.2. Suppose that $A \rightarrow B$ *holds, where* B *is composite. Then* $A \rightarrow E$ *also holds where* E *is any part of* B *(i.e., where either* $E \in B$ *or* $E \subset B$*).*

P.3. $A \rightarrow E$ *cannot hold if* E *is a component of* A.

Besides P.0, which is absolutely certain, none of the other principles makes any existence assertions whatever. P.1-P.3 are all universal conditional statements—propositions which affirm that, whenever and if ever certain conditions are obtained, then certain other conditions must be fulfilled. In other words, these statements in themselves have no existential import. However, in conjunction with P.0 (i.e., under the assumption that *something* exists), these principles have strong and somewhat surprising existential consequences.

> **Theorem.** *It follows from P.0-P.3 that there is one and only one self-caused phenomenon* G. *Further, this* G *is simple (non-composite) and is a (necessarily unique) universal cause (i.e., a cause of every existent phenomenon).*

> **Proof.** *We begin by asking the question "What is the cause of the global phenomenon* V*?" By P.1,* V *is either self-caused or other-caused. Suppose for the moment that it is self-caused,* $V \rightarrow V$. *By P.0,* V *is composite. Hence, there is some component* $E \in V$. *Therefore, by P.2,* $V \rightarrow E$. *But this contradicts the limitation principle P.3 since* E *is a component of* V. *Thus,* V *cannot be self-caused. In fact this argument is applicable to*

any composite and establishes the general principle: that no composite phenomenon can be self-caused.

Applying P.1 to the above, we now conclude that V must be other-caused by some phenomenon G ≠ V, G → V. Now, every phenomenon is either a component or a subsystem of V (see above). We thus have G → V and G is a part of V. By P.2, we can thus immediately conclude that G → G (i.e., G is self-caused). This means that G is simple because if G had some component E, we could then conclude (by P.2) that G → E, contradicting P.3. Thus, G is self-caused and simple. The simplicity of G implies that G is an entity (and thus a component of V, G ∈ V).

Moreover, G → V and every phenomenon B is a part of V. Hence, by P.2, G → B where B is any phenomenon whatever. G is therefore a universal cause.

Finally, G is the unique uncaused entity. To see this, suppose that G' → G' for some phenomenon G'. Now, we have already established that G is a universal cause, so G → G' also holds. Thus, G' is both self-caused and caused by G. However, P.1 asserts that no self-caused phenomenon can also be other-caused. Thus, G cannot be other than G' (i.e., G = G'). Hence, the simple entity G is the only uncaused phenomenon in existence.

It is important to realize that, in the light of the minimalistic method we have employed, the above theorem is not an idle word game. We have showed that the existence of a unique, simple, universal, uncaused cause follows by pure logic from a few, broad, objective properties of reality. In more formal terms, the conjuction of P.0-P.3 logically implies that G exits: (P.0 & P.1 & P.2 & P.3) ⟹ (G exists). This proof is totally objective. In other words, it is literally impossible that P.0-P.3 be true and that G not exist. Let us now take P.0 for granted.

Thus, anyone for whom the conclusion that G exists is unacceptable has only one rational course of action: he must deny one or more of P.1-P.3. This is not so simple and straightforward as may be imagined at first. To deny a proposition is to affirm its negation. The negation of any universal proposition is an existential proposition. Thus, pure logic dictates that, to deny that G exists, one must affirm the existence of a metaphysical phenomenon satisfying certain highly implausible conditions.

For example, if we deny P.3, then we affirm that, in objective fact, there is some composite phenomenon B that causes one of its own components. This is not only against logical intuition, it goes against every known or reported scientific observation of concrete systems. Similarly, if we deny P.2, then we are committed to belief in the existence of some system A which has caused the whole system B but which is not a cause of some proper part E of B. Again, such a configuration contradicts all of our current knowledge about the dynamics of systems.

Science is based on plausible reasoning. Such reasoning proceeds by always choosing the most plausible proposition in the light of known evidence. Each of P.1-P.3 is significantly (one is tempted to say infinitely) more plausible than its negation in the light of current knowledge. We can thus conclude that denial of the existence of G is irrational and unscientific. It contradicts the method of science because it involves deliberately choosing a less plausible alternative in order to avoid a specific conclusion.

To what extent are we justified in identifying our G with God? The answer, as we shall see, is that the justification is very great indeed. All traditions, whether philosophical, religious, or scientific, consider that God (if He exists) is, first and foremost, the Creator—the ultimate cause of all existence. We have proved that our G is in fact the one and only universal cause. This implies, in particular, that every concrete, observable phenomenon is the final step in a (possibly infinite) causal chain that begins with G.

Philosophy and metaphysics have considered that God's existence must be special or intrinsic, that God is self-sufficient—the only phenomenon whose existence is independent of anything else. Again, we have proved that our G is the only self-sufficient (self-caused) entity in existence. Other traditions (e.g., Islamic philosophical theology) have laid great emphasis on the unity of God—that the essence of God can admit of no division into parts. Again, we have proved that our G is a simple (and therefore indivisible) entity.

Of course, the prophetic religions in particular have also insisted that God is a living being and not just an ultimate principle. We have not yet proved this, but the strength of our minimalistic method is that it is forward compatible: the notion of God represented by the proved properties of our G are wholly compatible with such further properties.[54]

However, even without developing further proofs, we can draw certain conclusions from the fact that every major prophetic religion has identified their God as the ultimate origin of all existence. For example, the Hebrew Bible begins with the affirmation that "In the beginning God created the heavens and the earth," and continues by recounting how God made "every living creature that moveth."[55] Thus, whatever other attributes the Torah ascribes to the God of Israel (that He is their God, the God who spoke to and through Moses, a jealous God, etc.), He is and remains the God of Creation, the ultimate cause of all existence. But we have proved that there can only be one such ultimate cause of all existence. Hence, the God of Israel, if He exists, is our G.

In other words, as soon as we conceive of God as Creator, then whatever other attributes we may eventually wish to ascribe to God can apply only to our G, because in the light of principles P.1-P.3, it is not logically possible to have more than one Creator. This gives a new, logical meaning to monotheism.[56]

If we turn to Christianity, we can draw a similar conclusion. The Gospel of John presents Jesus Christ as the incarnation of the Logos (the Word made flesh) and the Logos as the divine agency through which "All things were made" and without whom "not anything made … was made" (John 1.1 and 1.3). The Logos itself is identified with God (John 1.1). Thus, the God of Christianity is identified as the ultimate cause and origin of all being. In the light of principles P.1-P.3, there is only one such entity, namely our G. So again, all other attributes that Christians attribute to God (e.g., that He loves us, saves us, guides us) must apply to our G.

The Qur'án, the holy book of Islam, likewise identifies Allah, the Merciful, the Compassionate, as the Creator of all existence.

Finally, the Bahá'í Writings quite explicitly identify the God of revelation and prophecy with the God of creation:

> Existence is of two kinds: one is the existence of God which is beyond the comprehension of man. He, the invisible, the lofty and the incomprehensible is preceded by no cause but rather is the Originator of the cause of causes. He, the Ancient, hath no beginning and is the all-independent. The second kind of existence is the human existence. It is … not ancient, is dependent and hath a cause to it.[57]

Of course, the G of our theorem has certain definite attributes, and not every conceivable notion of God is compatible with G. For example, the simplicity of G contradicts the conception of a Trinitarian God, at least as a metaphysical principle which sees God as consisting of three components. (There are other metaphorical interpretations of the Trinity which avoid this contradiction.) Also, the simplicity of God as a unique entity, noncomposite and distinct from other entities, definitely contradicts the cruder forms of pantheism which hold that everything that exists is a part of God (essentially the notion that V=G, i.e., that V is self-caused). In other words, our theorem shows that the theology of metaphysical trinitarianism and the theology of strict pantheism are logically incompatible with principles P.1-P.3. Thus, minimalistic metaphysics has implications for philosophical theology.

It might appear at first that the notion of God represented by our G is strictly Deistic (i.e., that it invokes God only as a first principle who has acted only once to launch the whole system of reality). However, a little reflection shows that things are not quite so simple. Indeed, one of the readings of the causality relation A→B is that "the phenomenon A represents the preconditions for the existence of B." Under this interpretation, G→G means that "the precondition for the existence of G is that G exists." Thus, once we have established that an uncaused G exists, it follows that it must have always existed and will always exist, because the only precondition for its existence is that it exist. (If there had ever been a period when it did not exist, then the condition of its existence could never have been satisfied so that it could engender itself.) If ever the condition of existence is satisfied, then it is always satisfied. (This recalls the words addressed by God to Moses: "I am that I am.") In other words, a self-caused entity either never exists or else exists always.

Self-causality implies not only eternality of existence but also eternality (or absoluteness) of state (i.e., that God is "unchanging"). Indeed, in any system, a change of state is itself a phenomenon which must have a cause. But G is not composite, and the only cause of G is G itself. Thus, G could only change if the cause of G changes (i.e., G can only change if G can change). G is thus either absolutely unchanging or continually changing in exactly the same way. Logically, these two conditions are equivalent. In the first case we conceive G to be static and, in the second, dynamic. But in neither case is there evolution or modification of state.[58]

In contemplating the fact that we have established such a controversial conclusion on the basis of such natural principles, one should recall our previous discussion concerning the power of logic to derive the unobvious from the obvious. Indeed, in the eyes of most people, our principles P.1-P.3 are so obvious as to be beyond serious controversy. Formulating them as explicit assumptions even appears at first to be a case of philosophical hairsplitting.

As a matter of fact, these principles are taken for granted in all the sciences. We have already shown that P.1 has been the basis of natural science—indeed of rationality itself—during two-thousand years of the development of Western science and philosophy. Similarly the componenthood relation is now known to be the ultimate basis of all mathematics.[59] We might think of the principles P.1-P.3 as constituting part of an indefinite list of general logico-empirical principles that underlie all of scientific or cognitive activity in whatever specific domain. These general principles articulate what we might call the overall or gross structure of reality.

This perspective gives a certain natural structure to metaphysics and epistemology. The most basic truths are the logical truths, which are absolutely objectifiable (see our previous discussion). Since logical truths are invariant under all *possible* lexical changes, they are, in Leibniz' sense, "true in all possible worlds" (cf. note 20).

Next in generality would be those principles whose articulation depends upon the fixed meaning of certain fundamental lexical terms (e.g., *cause of, component of*), and which are true only in a world (such as ours) where the particular meanings in question are realized. Included in this second level of generality would be truths which establish relationships between two or more of our fundamental notions (e.g., P.2 and P.3) and truths that establish intrinsic properties of a single fundamental notion (e.g., P.1). Mathematics would be included in this second level of generality since the principles of mathematics can all be expressed in a language whose only fixed lexical term is the componenthood relation $\in$.

The truths of the second level of generality would be common to all of the sciences. These global truths depend on the structure of reality, but only on the broad structure of reality as a whole, not on any particular feature of a limited part of reality. Finally, a third level of generality would be those truths which are *local* (i.e., which hold only under certain local conditions that will be satisfied only for systems of a specified type). Physical laws such as gravity or Archimedes' principle would be in this third category.[60]

Viewed in this framework, our theorem shows that the existence of God as a universal uncaused cause already follows from the global structure of reality as a whole. No recourse to the intricacies of such theories as quantum mechanics or general relativity is necessary in order to know that God exists.

Given the epistemological status of our theorem, one can wonder why such a clear proof has been so long in coming. The answer to this question is itself illuminating. Our theorem is a *cosmological* proof of God, so-called because it appeals to the extra-logical principle that something exists (our P.0). There is a continuous history of cosmological proofs, beginning with Aristotle's famous proof of an uncaused cause by appeal to a principle of infinite regress. However, the latter principle is open to serious debate and is provably false in the strong form articulated by Aristotle (an infinite regress is logically impossible), though arguably valid in a restricted form (an infinite regress of causes is impossible). More importantly, Aristotle establishes neither the uniqueness nor the universality of his uncaused cause. Thus, it is perfectly compatible with his proof that there be an infinity of different uncaused causes, none of which is universal.

The first substantial improvement over Aristotle was effected by Avicenna (980-1037), who eliminated completely the appeal to any principle of infinite regress. He did this by bringing in the potency principle (our P.2) and the whole relationship between cauality and composition. Aristotle's approach (to this question) had neglected composition altogether and focused on properties of the causality relation alone.

However, Avicenna's cosmological proof shares with other, later proofs the drawback of relying on modal logic. The classical logic that we have presented is based on only two things: grammatical structure (which can be made totally explicit) and the truth value (truth or falsity) of propositions. A logical truth is a true proposition that remains true under all possible reinterpretations of lexicon. In this logic, the validity of a logical principle can be detected in a purely formal manner, because grammatical form is invariant under changes of lexicon.

Modal logic, like mathematics or physics, makes essential use of a certain fixed part of the lexicon, in this case the lexical terms *necessary* and *possible*. In modal logic, one distinguishes between truth, necessary truth, and possible truth. In other words, it is no longer just the fact of being true that is important, but also the mode (quality) or degree of truth. The result is that there is no universally agreed upon system of modal logic. The use of modal logic introduces into logic the same degree of uncertainty that exists in, say, physics or psychology.

Our theorem is based quite closely on Avicenna's approach, but it eliminates completely the use of modalities. Of course, the self-caused G has a quality of existence that distinguishes it from other-caused phenomena. Some philosophers would say that self-causation represents *necessary* existence whereas other-causation is *contingent* or *possible* existence. However, Avicenna's use of modalities was more complicated and does not allow this reduction, because he recognized a difference between *necessary by reason of itself* and *necessary by reason of another*. He also had a third category of "possibly existing without necessity either by reason of self or of another." This brief reference should serve to give the reader some appreciation for the potential complexities of modalities and modal logic. Our way of eliminating completely the use of modal logic from Avicenna's proof appears to be original, but follows a suggestion made by Davidson.[61]

Some philosophers have contended that simple existence is not enough for God. Not only must He have supreme attributes, His very existence must be of a different quality. God, they say, must exist necessarily or not at all. For these philosophers, modal logic is an essential element of any valid proof of God's existence. Some would even go so far as to reject our proof because it only etablishes that a universal cause exists, but not that a universal cause *necessarily* exists (whatever that means).

The modal form of the cosmological proof has many variants, but it runs roughly as follows: Existence is either contingent (non-existence is equally possible) or necessary (non-existence is impossible). If all existence was contingent, then nothing would exist because there would be nothing to actualize the existence potential of contingents. But something does exist (our P.0, the mark of a cosmological proof). Thus, there must be a necessary existent that has actualized the existence potential of everything else. This necessary existent is God.

Insistence on proving God by the use of the modality of necessity is not only gratuitous and unclear, it can actually be turned into the following disproof of God: if God is the only phenomenon whose existence is necessary (whose non-existence is impossible), then God's existence should be the most undeniable of all existents. The mark of an undeniable proposition is that it tends to elicit assent on the part of most people. But the proposition that God exists is in fact quite controversial and is far from eliciting assent from people generally. Hence, God's existence is deniable and hence not necessary. Finally, according to the modal principle of necessary existence, God does not exist at all if His existence is not necessary. Hence, God does not exist.[62]

The superiority of Avicenna's proof over Aristotle's lies principally in Avicenna's use of both composition and causality, by which he appeals to the obvious potency principle in place of Aristotle's appeal to the doubtful/controversial infinite regression principle. Indeed, Avicenna's methods anticipate by a thousand years the development of the modern logic of relations.

Avicenna was quite aware of the novelty of his method, but saw it only as a new way of proving God's existence, not as part of a general (novel) logic. As an historical consequence, Avicenna's successors (e.g., Maimonides, Aquinus, Leibniz) either did not understand or did not appreciate the subtlety of Avicenna's method, and reformulated Avicenna's proof in Aristotlean terms (e.g., appealing to principles of infinite regression), but using modal logic. They therefore neglected Avicenna's essential advance in method while retaining the use of modalities which, as we have seen above, is really a regression.[63] Thus, most later versions of the cosmological proof have been along the lines we sketched three paragraphs above, and this version is subject to the Kantian antinomies.

The only modern philosopher who has taken a clear negative position with regard to any of the principles P.1-P.3 is Bertrand Russell who, in his debate with the Jesuit philosopher Copplestone, forthrightly denies the principle of sufficient reason P.1. Let us take a quick look at Russell's argument.

Causality, he says, is purely local in nature. The cause of any local phenomenon is some other local phenomenon. Thus, when we ask the question, "What is the cause of the global phenomenon V?" there is a subtle shift in the meaning of the word *cause*. Local causality is causality *within the system*, but now we are asking what is the cause *of the system itself*. This latter question, says Russell, is *meaningless*.

Thus, Russell denies P.1 not only by accepting that the universe of existence V is *without a cause* (either in itself or by something else), but also by denying us the right to ask the question as to whether V has or has not a cause. All talk of the ultimate origin of existence is neither true nor false but simply meaningless, according to Russell.[64]

The fundamental problem with Russell's position is that it is thoroughly irrational and unscientific. In our previous discussion, we have already pointed out that the principle of sufficient reason is the very basis of scientific rationality. It guarantees that the question *why?* is always meaningful. Science has been built on the foundation of this principle, and scientifically-minded philosophers have consistently exalted the principle of sufficient reason as representing the superiority of scientific thinking over superstitious thinking. Science, they insist, is not afraid to ask *why?*, but religion and superstition just say "that's the way it is, don't ask why." But these same supposed rationalists do not hesitate at an *ad hoc* derogation of the principle of sufficient reason in the one single instance in which the answer to the *why question* leads to a conclusion they do not like. Moreover, no logical basis is given for this derogation. Russell, for instance, simply proclaims the *why question* to be meaningless in this one particular instance. He does not attempt to give any logical justification as to why the question of global causality should be meaningless.[65]

A position similar to Russell's is taken by the cosmologist Stephen Hawking in his well-known work *A Brief History of Time*.[66] Hawking is the proponent (and to some extent the originator) of the so-called big bang cosmological theory. Retro-extrapolating from the fact that the observable space-time universe is expanding, Hawking and others have concluded that space-time sprang into being from a point (a so-called isolated singularity) some ten to twenty billion years ago. Hawkings is a materialist who believes that space-time is all of reality, V=Space-Time. He therefore assumes that all causality reduces to temporal causality. If,

further, we assume à la big bang that time itself had a discrete beginning, say fifteen billion years ago, then there cannot be any cause to this
event because there is no temporal *before* in which the cause could have
existed.

Thus, says Hawking, we simply have to accept the fact that the big
bang (and/or the big bang singularity) existed without a cause. In coming to this conclusion, Hawking does not explicitly discuss the possibility
of self-causality in relationship to the big bang. However, the composite
and evolutionary character of the universe (in particular the law of entropy) exclude self-causation, as we have already seen in our previous
discussion.

The weakness of Hawking's argument, as he himself acknowledges
explicitly, is that the very laws of physics (the causality relationships)
which predict the big bang singularity cease to hold at any singularity.
But the reasoning of two paragraphs above is based on these laws. There
is thus a *gap* or hiatus in this reasoning, and so the conception of a
(logical) cause for the big bang is wholly compatible with all of the
current laws of physics. Moreover, Hawking's assumptions that all reality is space-time and all causality temporal is question begging of the
worst sort. It excludes *a priori* the possibility of a non-physical dimension to reality and (à la Leibniz) of logical causality relations between
unobservable and observable reality.

Hawking's argument for the rejection of the principle of sufficient
reason is thus not compelled by logic, but represents rather his personal
preference in believing that the same physical laws must somehow still
hold even at singular points. In his discussion, Hawking even acknowledges that the *God hypothesis* may in fact be more reasonable than his
preferred materialistic alternative (which negates the principle of sufficient reason).

Hawking's position is actually quite similar to the one taken about
two-hundred years earlier by the skeptical philosopher David Hume,
who also assumed that the universe just sprang into existence without
any cause. Hume also made the reductionistic (and question-begging)
assumption that logical causality does not exist and that what we call
causality is just unwarranted extrapolation from temporal succession.
Of course Hawking's arguments are more scientifically sophisticated

than Hume's, given the intervening progress of physics. But philosophically and logically they are quite close.

Finally, let us mention, without going into detail, that all of Kant's so-called antinomies of reason involve reductionistic and/or question-begging assumptions which are totally inapplicable to the minimalistic approach of our theorem. In other words, the antinomial character of Kant's arguments are built into the very way they are constructed in the first place.

8. THE VALUE RELATION

We now consider a third binary relationship, the *value relation,* which only holds between (i.e., is meaningful for) entities. Where A and B are two entities, we write A≥B to mean that A is as valuable as B (i.e., the *intrinsic value* of A is greater than or equal to the *intrinsic value* of B). We write A>B to assert that the value of A is strictly greater than that of B (we say in this case the A is *higher* than B). We assume that the intrinsic value of an entity is inherent in the very nature and structure of the entity.

The defining characteristics of the value relation between two entities depends significantly on the ontological categories to which the entities belong. For example, for concrete composite (physical) entities, value is largely a function of complexity of structure, the higher value accruing to the more complex. Thus, plants are more complex and thus higher than minerals, animals more complex than plants, and (physically speaking) humans the most complex of all. Thus, viewed as a hierarchy of systems, the value of composite physical entities is more or less directly proportional to their degree of order or fineness of structure. In thermodynamic terms, the greater the distance from themodynamic equilibrium, the higher the value.

The value hierarchy of physical entities can also be characterized by the number and kinds of energy transformations of which they are capable. For example, a mineral such as a rock is essentially limited to absorbing and radiating energy. But a plant can also use energy to complexify its structure (i.e., to grow), and the higher animals are capable, further, of using energy for locomotion and for physical sensibilities such as sight and smell. Finally, humans can also process energy in the form of pure information, decoding and encoding abstract symbols and sounds (speech). This is clearly a cumulative hierarchy in which each higher entity can accomplish all the energy transformations of any lower entity, but not conversely.

Notice that the hierarchy of mineral, vegetable, animal, and human is precisely Aristotle's "chain of being." The difference, however, is that Aristotle was obliged to appeal to metaphysical (transempirical) notions to define his chain. Our objective and empirical definitions of the hierarchy of being are possible because of the vast increase in the sophistication of scientific knowledge since the time of Aristotle. Thus, once again, science gives us an empirical ground to a metaphysical notion—the notion of qualitative (value) differences between entities.

Between abstract entities, the value relation of greater to lesser is essentially the relationship between universal and particular. A universal will have every positive quality of a particular to the same or higher degree as the particular. Again, this is empirically grounded by the corresponding notion that higher physical entities can accomplish the types of energy transformations of lower ones, but not conversely.

Notice that we do not presume here (or elsewhere) that two given entities are necessarily comparable with respect to value. That is, it is quite conceivable, for entities A and B, that neither $A \geq B$ nor $B \geq A$ holds. We also allow for the possibility that two different entities can have the same value (i.e., $A \geq B$, $B \geq A$, and $A \neq B$). (Thus, two different dogs or two different human beings could be of equal value).

The branch of philosophy called *ethics* is the study of the properties of the value relationship. In a recent work, *Love, Power, and Justice,* we have presented our own analysis of the value relationship.[67] In the present text, we are mainly concerned about the logical connections between the three relations of value, causality, and componenthood. In fact, we will explicitly assume only one further principle, *the refinement principle,* which links causality with value:

P.4. Where A and B are entities, if $A \rightarrow B$, then $A \geq B$.

Principle P.4 says that, where entities are concerned, a lower thing cannot be the cause of a higher thing: only something of equal or higher value can be the cause of a given entity.

This last principle is also empirically grounded. Indeed, if A and B are composite physical entities, then P.4 is precisely the second law of thermodynamics. For physical entities, the causality of B by A implies a transfer or flow of energy from A to B. In such a case there can be dissipation of energy and loss of order, but (by the law of entropy) never increase in energy or complexification of structure. Thus, if B is an effect of the cause A, then A must have equal or greater complexity than B, which is precisely what A≥B means for physical composite entities.

The principle of refinement P.4 is thus the generalization to all entities (including abstract entities) of an established scientific principle that holds for concrete composite entities. It gives precise expression to the traditional philosophical notion that *the cause is greater than its effect*. We can now draw corollaries to our theorem.

Corollary 1. *God is the supreme good, the most valuable entity in existence.*

Proof. *By our theorem, God is the universal cause. Thus, for every phenomenon A, G→A. But an entity is a phenomenon. Thus, G→A holds for every entity A. Hence, by P.4, G≥A for every entity A (i.e., God is the most valuable entity in existence).*

In particular, God is more valuable than every human being H, since G→H and thus G≥H. This means that God has every positive (abstract) quality of any given human being. Each individual human has such positive qualities as consciousness, intelligence, compassion or will to a specific, finite, and limited degree. However, there is no limit to the degree that these qualities can exist generally in human beings. But God is the single creator not just of each human being but of all humanity. Thus, God must have these qualities to a degree that is beyond every finite or limited degree, thus to an infinite, unlimited degree. God is thus infinitely intelligent, loving, powerful, etc. In fact, since God is the only entity whose existence is absolute (uncaused), then it is reasonable to suppose that God has these qualities to an absolute degree. Thus, the logical answer to the question "what is God's nature?" is to say that "God is like us except for possessing none of our limitations and all of our positive abstract qualities to an infinite degree." Of course, we cannot really imagine what it means to possess such qualities as consciousness or will to an infinite degree, but the refinement principle does nevertheless give us at least a minimal, purely logical, notion of God's nature.

It is important to realize that this way of reasoning about God's nature is not anthropomorphism (i.e., creating God in our image). Anthroporphism results when we project all of our qualities onto God— both our limitations and our strengths. We then see God as having such negative qualities as jealousy, petulance, vengefulness, etc.

For further development of the minimalist method applied to ethics and the value relation, the interested reader can consult the author's *Love, Power, and Justice* cited above.

VI. CONCLUSION AND SUMMARY

In the course of this monograph, we have threaded our way through a series of bifurcations, starting with the most basic of all questions, the question of the existence of an objective, mind-independent reality, and ending up with the existence and nature of God. At each stage of this process, we have carefully considered the basic alternatives, and in each case we have determined that one of them was clearly and significantly more plausible than the others. The philosophy that results from consistently making the most plausible and rational choice in the light of our current knowledge, is what we have called minimalism.

The minimalistic method avoids reductionism in several respects. In the first place, it is empirically based, and so does not presume that what is the most rational choice in the light of currently known evidence will always be the most rational choice. It is therefore an open philosophy, not a dogmatic one. In the second place, minimalism does not suppose that all humanly knowable truth can be obtained by this method. For example, the philosophy of minimalism is open to the possibility of such phenomena as divine revelation, in which man may be given knowledge that transcends any possible rational basis that is currently known. Minimalism likewise acknowledges that intuition and mysticism may give rise to transrational modes of knowing reality. But minimalism does not accept that either divine revelation or mysticism can contradict the conclusions of reason *in the face of the same information base.* For minimalism, there is a fundamental and important difference between that which transcends reason and that which contradicts reason—between the transrational and the irrational. Thirdly, minimalism makes no gratuitous or *a priori* assumptions, such as the assumption that all of reality is contained within space-time or that there are no causality relations between nonphysical and physical phenomena.

In undertaking this exposition, we have sought to show both by positive example and by critical analysis of classical and modern philosophy, that a truly non-reductionistic rationalism is possible and productive. We have seen that such an approach can go well beyond the gratuitous restrictions of materialism and logical positivism without falling into the excesses of subjectivism and postmodernism. We have also seen that, contrary to the presumption of many, a non-dogmatic rationalism does not favor skepticsm, cynicism, atheism, or even agnosticism with regards to such fundamental life questions as the existence and nature of God.

Minimalism is thus a *middle way* between the gratuitous restrictions of logical positivism, which have been uncritically accepted by many as essential to rational philosophy, and the gratuitous subjectivism of postmodernism, which willfully abandons the discipline of reason and logic. Postmodernism has presented itself as freedom from what it calls "the tyranny of reason." What we have shown is that this is the freedom of anarchy and stagnation, whereas the discipline of reason gives us the freedom of intellectual autonomy and the benefit of observable individual and social progress.

NOTES AND REFERENCES

1. See K. Gödel, *Collected Works,* Vol. 1, Oxford University Press, New York, 1986, pp. 144-195.

2. R. Penrose, *Shadows of the Mind,* Oxford University Press, Oxford, 1994.

3. 'Abdu'l-Bahá, *Some Answered Questions,* Bahá'í Publishing Trust, Willmette, 1984, p. 221. 'Abdu'l-Bahá (1844-1921) is the eldest son of Bahá'u'lláh (1817-1892), founder of the Bahá'í Faith. In his Will and Testament, Bahá'u'lláh designated 'Abdu'l-Bahá as his successor and authorized interpreter of his writings. 'Abdu'l-Bahá wrote a number of philosophical treatises and commentaries, and we will have occasion to quote from several of them in the course of this monograph.

4. In *Zen and the Art of Motorcycle Maintenance,* Robert Pirsig recounts his tortuous philosophical journey, which took him to India for ten years where he studied Oriental Philosophy at Benares Hindu University. Pirsig describes his ultimate break with this philosophy in the following manner, referring to himself in the third person as *Phaedrus:*

    "But one day in the classroom the professor of philosophy was blithely expounding on the illusory nature of the world for what seemed the fiftieth time and Phaedrus raised his hand and asked coldly if it was believed that the atomic bombs that had dropped on Hiroshima and Nagasaki were illusory. The professor smiled and said yes. That was the end of the exchange."

    "Within the traditions of Indian philosophy that answer may have been correct, but to Phaedrus and anyone else who reads newspapers regularly and is concerned with such things as mass destruction of human beings that answer was hopelessly inadequate. He left the classroom, left India and gave up." (p. 144.)

5. 'Abdu'l-Bahá, *Some Answered Questions,* p. 251.

6. As good a philosopher as John Locke succumbed to this confusion, holding that our own ideas and feelings are the only thing we really know, because our immediate experience is only of our own ideas and feelings. He fell into this view because he was a *radical empiricist* who believed that experience and knowledge are identical. Since our immediate *experience* is always of our own thoughts and feelings, Locke concluded (falsely) that our *knowledge* is only of our own thoughts and feelings. For Locke, the mind is only a blank slate on which experience writes—a passive recipient of experience rather than an active processor of experience.

7. A fairly comprehensive treatment of epistemology can be found in the author's previous works: *The Science of Religion,* Association for Bahá'í Studies, Ottawa, 2nd edition, 1980; *Logic and Logos,* George Ronald, Oxford, 1990; *The Law of Love Enshrined,* George Ronald, Oxford, 1996.

8. To say otherwise would be to affirm the obvious absurdity that you are infallible, that all your ideas and conceptions—from your most casual assumptions about who

is faithful in love to your most speculative beliefs about the cosmos—are totally free from error.

9. The positivist viewpoint is sometimes incorrectly formulated by the slogan that "reality is not observer-independent." Of course, those realities related to our actions do depend on us, but in general it is not reality but verification that is partially dependent on the observer.

10. The positivist-deconstructionist approach in physics is illustrated by Niels Bohr's operationalist interpretation of quantum mechanics. Bohr apparently held that quantum events existed only when they were measured—that the quantum measures (verifications) were the only quantum reality.

11. Notice that the entity that is posited as an end (or solution) to the infinite regress of causes is a first (uncaused) cause. Uncausedness is one of the attributes that classical theology attributes to God. Hence, in dealing with the question of an infinite regress of causes, we do have to make a logical choice between accepting that such an infinite regress can indeed exist, or else accepting the existence of a nonobservable entity which has one of the major attributes of God as conceived by classical theology.

12. Notice that the end (solution) to the infinite regress of verifications is a mind capable of absolute certainty, again a classical attribute of God.

13. Kuhn, *The Structure of Scientific Revolutions,* University of Chicago Press, Chicago, 1962.

14. This was demonstrated by the mathematician Alan Sokal, who successfully published as a serious article in the journal *Social Text* a completely phony piece in which he made various absurd claims, for example that physical reality is nothing but a social construct. After exposing the hoax, he commented on the state of affairs which allowed supposedly serious scholars to accept such absurdities as statements of fact. See Sokal, Transgressing the boundaries: Toward a transformative hermeneutics of quantum gravity, *Social Text,* Vol. 46/47, 1996, pp. 217-252; Sokal and Bricmont, *Impostures intellectuelles,* Odile Jacob, 2nd edition, Paris, 1999.

15. According to our definition, text (discourse) can be either written or verbal. In the beginning period of modern linguistics, verbal discourse was considered the primary or authentic form of linguistic expression, and written text was considered to be only a secondary transcription of speech. However, once it was realized that spoken language has a syntactic structure essentially identical to written language (e.g., where phonemes play the role of alphabetic letters), this difference began to lose its importance. The successful invention and proliferation of formal and artificial languages made it clear that nothing was lost by considering all forms of discourse/text as equally authentic.

16. The mathematical theory of information gives a precise form to this truth via the following theorem: there can be no transfer of information without the generation of noise. Of course, we can reduce the ratio of noise to information, but never

eliminate noise entirely. Notice also that the end (solution) to the infinite regress of language, meta-languages, meta-meta-languages, etc., would be an entity capable of perfect or absolute communication. Such an entity would in fact be the very incarnation of the word or *logos,* yet another divine attribute.

17. As our discourse progresses, the characteristic pattern of the minimalist approach to philosophy begins to emerge: relative truth does not mean no truth; relative verification does not mean total uncertainty; relative objectivity does not mean total subjectivity. Indeed, many classical and contemporary problems in philosophy have been generated by a tendency to *all-or-nothing* on both sides of the debate. In each case, either extreme position has weak points which proponents of the opposite extreme can exploit to advance their claims, and either extreme has some truth which attracts a certain contingent of serious-minded people to that position. As long as each side talks past the other by focusing only on the other's weakest points, each side can remain secure in the sense that what it says is clearly true. Those who, like myself, attempt to find a more satisfactory position that avoids either extreme are usually perceived by both sides as traitors to the truth (and indeed such *reasonable* positions do undermine the (absolute) *truth* as perceived by each extreme position).

In the minimalist perspective, such reasonable positions are not intermediates or compromises between two extremes. More precisely, minimalism considers philosophy not as a dialogue of persuasion between different opinions but rather as a dialogue between ourselves (individually and collectively) and reality, a dialogue whose goal is to find the truth (i.e., to construct the most accurate model possible). Whether or not others are persuaded by minimalist arguments is strictly a secondary consideration. Minimalism focuses on the intrinsic integrity of the philosophic enterprise, not its acceptability in the eyes of one or another dogmatic position.

18. Notice that we have yet another classical attribute of God: total awareness, a form of omniscience.

19. The notion of completeness involved here can be made quite precise. The fundamental point is that new connectors can be constructed by appropriate combinations of the basic ones. Moreover, even our basic set is not minimal in this regard: some of them can be defined by appropriate combinations of the others.

20. The use of the terms grammar and grammatical form in this section might appear somewhat nonstandard to linguists. Our usage here conforms to that of other logicians such as Quine (see, Quine, *Philosophy of Logic,* Prentice-Hall, Englewood Cliffs, 1970). Since we make our definition totally explicit, there should be no cause for confusion with other connotations of these terms.

Logical truth is sometimes informally characterized as *truth in all possible worlds.* As it stands, such a characterization is incorrect, because it is quite possible to have a world in which there is no language as we know it, and thus no grammatical form, and thus no logical truth. However, given a language L in the world that we do in fact have, then a logical truth is indeed invariant under *all possible* reinterpretations of its lexicon. It should be clear that reinterpretations of lexicon can only take place within a given lexical category, never from one category to another.

21. Because logical truth is preserved under similarity of grammatical form, some have drawn the conclusion that a logical truth is true *by virtue of* its grammatical form alone, but this is a serious mistake. A proposition is true because what it affirms about reality is in fact the case, and a logical truth is first of all a truth. "John is John" is true because in fact any human being, John in particular, is the same as him(her-)self. The universality of self-identity is a fact, and this fact allows us to recognize that any English statement of the form "A is A", where A is a substantive, is true. In other words, the fact that we may be able to *recognize* a logical truth by its form doesn't mean that it is true *because of* its form.

   Or put it another way: truth is a semantic notion and so logical truth is a semantic notion. Once we have defined logical truth (true and truth-invariant under lexical reinterpretation), we then observe that, in fact, logical truth is preserved under similarity of grammatical form. This latter is thus a property of logical truth, not a definition of logical truth. Logical truth, like all truth, is thus grounded in empirical reality. This point will become extremely important in our subsequent development, and failure to understand it has been the cause of considerable philosophical misery for many people.

22. Again we can generalize as in the above and say that, where P is any proposition, the complex proposition having the form "If P then P" will be true regardless of the truth value (truth or falsity) of P. In other words, "If P then P" is a logical truth, for any proposition P.

23. *Formalization* is the process of presenting the grammar of a language in totally explicit form. The language L thus presented is said to be *formalized.* Formalization should not be confused with the reductionist philosophy called *formalism,* which holds that any semantic or linguistic notion is incoherent unless it can be formalized. In other words, formalism attempts to reduce the whole of language to that part which can be made totally explicit. Minimalism embraces the usefulness of formal methods, but recognizes that the totality of linguistic reality cannot be formalized.

   Some philosophers like to dismiss the *merely formal* as the product of soulless, poetically insensitive human machines. However, formalization has very great practical applications with an immense potential for alleviating much human misery. Indeed, the fact that grammatical form can be made totally explicit is the only thing that allows us to build and use electronic computing devices. Since a computer is utterly devoid of consciousness and thus of subjectivity, it cannot read lexical meaning. It can, however, read formal meaning (i.e., that part of the meaning which can be completely formalized—that is, the part of meaning which can be made explicit in grammatical form alone).

   Although computers have clear limitations, both practical and theoretical (see note 24), we have all been surprised by the extent to which meaning can be formalized.

The success of formalization, and of electronic computers in particular, constitutes irrefutable evidence that grammatical form can indeed be made totally explicit. In the same way that the Newton-Einstein theory of gravity is concrete evidence that convergence can and does occur in the pursuit of knowledge, so the successful construction and implementation of electronic digital computing devices is concrete evidence that a significant proportion of linguistic meaning can be made totally explicit and objective. Those who feel threatened by this fact are probably reacting to the formalistic philosophy of many computer scientists, who personally believe in the reductionistic proposition that there is nothing to language beyond what can be formalized. Minimalism embraces the reality of formalization but rejects the gratuitous reductionistic philosophy of formalism.

24. Since grammar can be made totally explicit, there exist computational algorithms that can recognize mechanically whether or not a given expression is meaningful (grammatically well-formed). However, since 1936 it has been known and proved (by A. Church) that there cannot exist, even in principle, an algorithm that will recognize computationally whether or not a given proposition is a logical truth. We say that the class of logical truths is *(computationally) undecidable.* The class of logical truths is nevertheless *semidecidable* in that there do exist algorithms with the following property: if we apply the algorithm to a proposition, and the algorithm terminates, then we know certainly that the proposition is a logical truth. If, however, the algorithm does not terminate, then we cannot conclude one way or the other.

   The possibility of the non-termination of algorithms for the class of logical truths comes from the requirement that logical truths be invariant under all possible lexical reinterpretations. In some cases, the possible reinterpretations are infinite in such a way that the computer (whether human or machine) will simply continue forever. Logical truth thus provides an example of a notion which is absolutely determined without being totally explicit (computable). However, there does exist a totally explicit set of rules and axioms for generating the set of logical truths.

25. If an L-proposition P is not logically false, then it must be true for at least one lexical interpretation. In this case, we say that P is *satisfiable.* If P is not logically true, then it must be false for at least one lexical interpretation. In this case, we say P is *falsifiable.* Thus, any proposition is either satisfiable but not falsifiable (logically true), falsifiable but not satisfiable (logically false), or both satisfiable and falsifiable (neither logically true nor logically false). Since by definition a proposition makes an affirmation about reality, any proposition must have a *truth value* (i.e., be either false or true) and thus be either satisfiable or falsifiable.

26. 'Abdu'l-Bahá, *The Tablet of the Universe,* unpublished English translation, Haifa, 1995, p. 4.

27. We use the ampersand, &, to symbolize the logical connector of conjunction, *and.* We also extend the turnstile symbol $\vdash$ to apply to deductions from finite sets of propositions. Thus, $\{P_1, ..., P_n\} \vdash Q$ means the same thing as $(P_1 \& P_2 \& ... \& P_n) \vdash Q$ (equivalently, $(P_1 \& P_2 \& ... \& P_n) \Rightarrow Q$).

28. We symbolize the logical connector *not* by $\neg$.

29. Indeed, if the P_i are inconsistent, then $(P_1 \& P_2 \& \ldots \& P_n)$ is logically false, making the proposition $((P_1 \& P_2 \& \ldots \& P_n) \supset (P \& (\neg P)))$ logically true (remember, a logical falsity implies anything). Hence, $(P_1 \& P_2 \& \ldots \& P_n) \Rightarrow (P \& (\neg P))$ which, by the completeness of our rules, yields $(P_1 \& P_2 \& \ldots \& P_n) \vdash (P \& (\neg P))$.

30. We can even extend the notions of logical consistency and inconsistency to infinite sets of propositions: a set X of propositions is consistent if and only if every finite subset of X is consistent. Or, equivalently, X is inconsistent if and only if some finite subset of X is inconsistent.

31. Notice an important logical point here. No amount of defects in your system will remove any defects that really exist in my system. Thus, the fact that I may refute your system and thereby win the argument of persuasion does not in itself bring me any closer to the truth of the matter. This simple point illustrates the uselessness of disputatious dialogue as a method of finding truth or communicating objectively.

32. 'Abdu'l-Bahá, *The Tablet of the Universe,* unpublished English translation, Haifa, 1995, p. 7.

33. Our analysis of logical truth draws heavily on the work of the leading American philosopher W. V. Quine. It is his persistent, meticulous, and careful analysis of these issues that has shown the way to all of us.

34. In particular, our analysis shows irrefutably that the importance of logic in the epistemological enterprise does not depend upon any notion of logical apriorism. This is important in the present philosophical climate, because many postmodernists have dismissed logic by claiming (falsely and without justification) that some doctrine of apriorism is a necessary adjunct to the application of logic to empirical reality.

Notice that a logical implication $P \Rightarrow Q$ also establishes an empirical truth: that whenever the empirical conditions described by P occur, then the configuration described by Q must also occur. In other words, implication is the counterpart, in our inner model, of the objective relationship of cause-and-effect in empirical reality. So we may gain knowledge of a causal relation in reality by pure logic and not just by empirical observation of concomitant variations between two phenomena. This point will be amplified in a later discussion.

35. Moreover, there are rational criteria for deciding which propositions should be dropped from an inconsistent theory. See W. S. Hatcher, A certain measure of importance, *Pensée naturelle, logique et langage,* Droz, Geneva, 1987, pp. 61-73.

36. 'Abdu'l-Bahá, *Some Answered Questions,* pp. 208-209.

37. See Jacques Bouveresse, *Prodiges et vertiges de l'analogie,* Éditions raisons d'agir, Paris, 1999, for a competent discussion of various postmodernist misuses of Gödel's theorem, with references to works of postmodernist authors.

38. Computerization is the ultimate test of objectification, because we know the computer lacks consciousness and is therefore devoid of subjectivity. For example, algorithmic (mechanical) procedures for calculation have been known since ancient times. But as long as their use was ultimately in the hands of humans, it was difficult to be certain that some degree of self-awareness was not necessary to their successful deployment. Of course, even with computers we must not forget that it is the human mind that builds them, repairs them, programs them, and interprets the results of their actions.

39. See Richard Dedekind, *Was Sind und Was Sollen die Zahlen?*, Braunschweig (6th ed. 1930), English translation in *Essays on the Theory of Numbers,* Open Court, Chicago, 1901 (reprinted, 1963).

40. Whereas observation statements will usually involve only concrete terms (i.e., those which refer to observable entities and configurations), the general propositions will often contain abstract terms (i.e., terms referring to nonobservable entities or forces).

41. Notice that there may not be any deductive links whatever between the facts themselves. In particular, this will be the case whenever our observations are all *independent* of each other.

42. We sketch the proof. First, we appeal to a well-known Lemma of predicate logic which affirms that if a proposition P is deductively undecided by a theory T (neither P nor $\neg P$ are theorems of T), then we can consistently extend T by adding either P or $\neg P$ as a new axiom. Let us call these extensions T_1 and T_2 respectively. Clearly T_1 and T_2 are logically incompatible, because T_1 affirms P whereas T_2 affirms its negation $\neg P$. Yet, both are consistent (non-contradictory and thus true under some appropriate lexical interpretation).

Now, given the body of facts (accumulated observation statements), let us consider the theory T generated by taking these facts as axioms. Since we are constructing a scientific theory, we can assume that T is sufficiently rich. Moreover, T is consistent unless some of the observation statements logically contradict each other. But this could happen only if objective reality actually contradicts itself, or else if some of our observation statements are inaccurate. This first case we reject as highly unreasonable. The second case is always a possibility, but let us assume that our observations are, in the given instance, reasonably accurate. Thus, T is a consistent, sufficiently rich, finitely-axiomatized (and thus objectively specifiable) system. Hence, by Gödel's incompleteness theorem, there is at least one proposition P in the language L that is deductively undecided by the theory T. But, by our Lemma, we can consistently extend T by adding either P or $\neg P$ as a new axiom, obtaining the incompatible theories T_1 and T_2 both of which are consistent extensions of T and thus, by definition, possible explanations for the original body of facts that constitutes the axioms of T. But, each of T_1 and T_2 contains a finite number of axioms, namely the original axioms plus the one new axiom P (respectively, $\neg P$). Thus, each of T_1 and T_2 will satisfy the hypotheses of Gödel's theorem, and likewise generate deductively undecidable propositions Q_1 and Q_2 respectively.

This process can be repeated indefinitely, and each time we will have, for each branch of the process, a binary choice of consistent extensions. No two of these branches can yield compatible theories, since each branch will contain at least one proposition which is the negation of some proposition on any other branch. There is thus an infinity of pairwise incompatible (and thus essentially different) logically possible explanations for the original body of facts. Thus, there cannot exist any rule of inductive logic that will lead us from the given finite body of facts to a unique generalization of these facts.

Could there be some natural way of eliminating all but a few of these possible explanations? Could it perhaps be that there is some one universal principle P from which the facts can be deduced and which is maximally general so as to be uniquely determined by the facts? The answer is no, because the addition of this universal principle would still constitute a finitely-axiomatized extension of the original fact-theory, and thus be logically independent of some deductively undecidable proposition Q. Each of the propositions P&Q or P&($\neg$Q) would then constitute a consistent, single principle, more general that P itself, from which the original fact-theory could be deduced. But these two propositions are logically incompatible, and so cannot both be legitimately regarded as inductive consequences of the same fact-theory. Yet, each of these propositions is logically compatible with the original fact-theory, and each equally satisfies all of the criteria for a putative inductive consequence of the fact-theory.

43. See W. V. Quine, *Word and Object,* MIT Press, Cambridge, Mass., 1980, p. 78.

44. Indeed, Einstein explains that he arrived at his general theory of relativity precisely by seeking to conserve as much as possible of the Newtonian approach (see his "Notes on the origin of the general theory of relativity" in *Essays in Science,* Wisdom Library, New York, 1934). In particular, by maintaining the Newtonian principle of the equality of inertial mass and gravitational mass, while accommodating invariance under uniformly accelerated relative motion, Einstein was led directly to the curvature of the geodesics in Riemannian space-time, with its non-Euclidean metric. Thus, however complex the theory of general relativity may be (and it is very complex), it was nonetheless discovered by pursuing a principle of simplicity (i.e., the conservation of as much of background Newtonian theory as possible).

45. Science is constantly walking a tightrope between the reductionist fallacy on one hand and the simplicity principle on the other. Suppose I come up with a beautifully simple generalized theory that explains not quite all of the fact-theory. There will be a very strong temptation to try to reduce the unexplained facts to others that are explained by the generalized theory. This temptation will be especially strong if the only generalized theories known to be adequate for the whole of the fact-theory are considerably more complicated than my beautifully simple but not quite adequate theory.

46. A typical example is afforded by much of the current debate on evolutionary theory. We now have overwhelming evidence that we cannot explain the origin and progression of life forms by chance alone. The only plausible conclusion is that there is

some force that has caused this progression (i.e., this persistent movement towards increased complexity and order), but many philosophical materialists still take the position that, even if chance (randomness) is the least probable explanation, it is still logically *possible,* and therefore a legitimate explanation for evolution.

The logic of plausibility is the essence of rationality. Deliberately to choose a less probable explanation over a more probable one is a serious derogation of scientific method and indeed of rationality itself. If the scientific community permitted such derogations freely, the scientific enterprise would soon be transformed into rampant mythmaking. Everyone would put forth his favorite theories on the basis of his emotional proclivities rather than on the basis of their plausibility. See my essay "Myths, models, and mysticism" in *Logic and Logos,* op. cit., for a more detailed discussion of this point.

The theory of plausible reasoning I have elaborated in this section has echoes in the work of contemporary philosophers of science (see, e.g., Newton-Smith, *The Rationality of Science,* Routledge, London, 1999; Christopher Norris, *Against Relativism,* Blackwell, Oxford, 1997; Alexander Bird, *Philosophy of Science,* McGill-Queen's University Press, Montreal & Kingston, 2000.) My account here is perhaps more precise but also somewhat more technical than these other authors.

47. The basic problem of metaphysics is determining the relationship between being and becoming, between existence and transformation of existents, between stasis and change. There are fundamentally two possible approaches. The first, and most frequent, is to take being as basic and to see process as a succession of *states,* a state being defined as a (time-bound) existent at a given instant of time. The second is to take process itself as basic, and then to see being as an underlying aspect of process. In the modern period, the second approach is most closely associated with the work of Alfred North Whitehead. Our minimalism is clearly within the first tradition.

Indeed, if we are certain of anything, it is that existence itself is not an illusion. But our perceptions of reality, including our perception of change, could well be illusory. Thus, from a minimalist perspective, the fact of existence (being) is more fundamental than is change (becoming). Hence, the notion of being is a more rational and minimalist basis for metaphysics than is the notion of becoming.

48. Indeed, one of the basic open questions of metaphysics is whether global connections exist (i.e., whether every aspect of existence is connected in some way with every other aspect of existence). Most philosophers find a positive answer to this question more attractive, but it is *a priori* logically possible that connections between existents are only local and limited and that reality is composed of a number of worlds that exist in parallel to each other. Our definitions and assumptions are agnostic on this issue.

49. I am convinced that many of the seemingly intractable problems of classical metaphysics result from various derogations of this principle. Some authors would consider what we have called concrete reality to be co-extensive with material or physical reality. But then, one has the problem of how to deal with objective nonobservables

such as the force of gravity. Are such forces nonmaterial? Others would go the other way, and declare everything objective to be material, whether observable or not. This takes care of gravity, but what about the force of love or the human soul. Are they material? Some would say *yes* but then they face the problem of trying to explain these things in material terms. Finally, if one takes the position that all of concrete reality is material but that nonobservable reality is partly spiritual and partly physical, then one has the problem of defining the difference between the nonobservable and physical (e.g., gravity) and the nonobervable and spiritual (e.g., love).

All of these positions involve strong metaphysical assumptions that are either materialistic, idealistic, or Platonistic. We avoid the whole thing simply by not attempting to make any logical distinction between material and spiritual at all. We retain only the distinction between observable and nonobservable, which is clearly empirically grounded if anything is. (The very hardest of modern physics makes a distinction between observables and nonobservables.)

However, in our informal discussions of reality, we will appeal to various examples drawn from modern physical theory. In these cases, we will freely use the terms *material* and *physical* in the sense that they are currently used and meant in the science of physics. This is not part of our metaphysics proper, but only constitutes examples and analogies to better understand the empirical ground of certain metaphysical concepts.

50. Note that $B \subset B$ holds by definition for any composite B, since, trivially, every component of B is a component of B. Also, by definition (cf. p. 85), $B \in B$ never holds. This, then, is another logical difference between componenthood and containment: containment is reflexive but componenthood is not. If $A \subset B$ and $A \neq B$, we say that A is a *proper* subsystem of B. Components are automatically proper since $A \in B$ only when $A \neq B$. By a *proper part* of B we mean a phenomenon A which is either a component or a proper subsystem of B.

51. A biological system is a collection of organs which function together to accomplish a specific vital function of an organism of which they are a part. Examples are the digestive system, the nervous system, or the circulatory system. An arbitrary collection of organs, say the brain and the large right toe, would consitute a portion of the body as an organism, but would not constitute a component. The human body is an archetypical example of a *modular system,* where larger components (systems and organs) are built from smaller components (organs and tissues, respectively), starting with the ultimate organic components (in this case, differentiated cells).

52. A leaved tree also has a modular structure, beginning with differentiated cells. Since each leaf functions independently of other leaves, the collection of leaves forms a subsystem of the tree, but does not constitute a component of the tree.

53. Another aspect of the debate about causality derives from the presumption by many philosophers (and in particular Hume and Kant) that causality between objective phenomena necessarily involves temporal succession. When combined with the as-

sumption (tentative in Descartes but explicit in his successor Leibniz) that there can be no non-material causes for material events, we obtain the view that the cause for any material event can only be another material event which preceeds it in time. (By an *event* we mean a time-parametered phenomenon—a phenomenon that is wholly within time). Further, for a materialist who believes that all of reality is contained within space-time, the causality relationship itself can only occur within space-time (i.e., between temporally successive material events).

Our approach, and our assumptions, are completely agnostic on these points. We do not presume, explicitly or implicitly, that there is in fact a non-material dimension to reality, and we do not exclude this possibility either. However, all our definitions and assumptions take into account the *possibility* that a substantial portion of reality may well be non-material. Hence, we adopt neither the Leibnizian assumption that material events must have material causes, nor the Humean assumption that the notion of causality necessarily presupposes temporal succession, nor the materialist assumption that all of reality is contained within space-time.

Thus, in our view, causality is first and foremost a *logical relationship* (B exists by virtue of A). Such a relationship may well imply temporal succession if A and B are material events, but we do not assume such succession to be a necessary (logical) aspect of causality. In the light of our approach, many of the classical problems of causality (e.g., those advanced by Kant in his discussion of the so-called antinomies of reason) can be seen to derive from the question-begging assumptions that reduce causality to a temporally successive relationship between material events.

54. This is yet another example of the difference between reductionism and minimalism. We have established a positive proof that our G satisfies certain attributes of God. But our G is not limited or restricted (reduced) to these properties alone. The notion of God represented by our G is thus compatible with the attribution of other, more personal qualities to God. Our proof, as it currently stands, is simply agnostic about these other attributes; it does not exclude them.

55. *The Holy Bible,* Genesis 1.1 and 1.21.

56. This illustrates the difference between a *logical definition*, which determines an entity uniquely, and a *comprehensive definition,* which defines an entity by giving all of its attributes. Thus, God is logically definable as the unique uncaused entity or the unique universal cause, but neither of these definitions allows us to deduce all of the other attributes of God. Traditional philosophy and metaphysics have often attempted to give comprehensive definitions. Our technique of beginning with a purely logical definition and then using further arguments to determine other attributes is an essential part of the method of minimalism.

57. See 'Abdu'l-Bahá, *Selections from the Writings of 'Abdu'l-Bahá,* Bahá'í Publishing Trust, Wilmette, Ill., 1997, no. 30.1.

58. Such a dynamic (non-static) stability can be approximated even in complex physical systems through the phenomenon of *convergence towards a fixed point.* For

example, under ideal conditions of health, the proportions of certain constituent elements of the human body may remain fixed even though the actual quantity of each individual substance is continually changing as a result of ongoing chemical reactions. This equilibrium is maintained by means of compensating reactions. Suppose, for example that $(A+B)+C$ yields $(D+E)+C$, while $(D+C)+E$, yields $(A+B)+C$. (We are thus supposing, as a contrived example, that C catalyses the forward reaction while E catalyses the reverse reaction.) Then, both the forward and the reverse reactions will be ongoing. If the rates of these reactions satisfy certain properties, and the initial quantities are within certain bounds, the proportions of some of these substances may remain constant throughout the process. Perhaps, for example, as soon as certain quantities of A and B combine in the presence of C to produce D and E, equivalent amounts of A and B are synthesized by the reverse reaction of D and C in the presence of E. Such reactions have been observed and studied by scientists (e.g., Prigogine), and also give rise to phenomenona known as *chemical clocks,* in which the concentrations of the substances vary in a regular manner within fixed limits (periodically).

Of course, for physical systems, such regularity of behavior can only be maintained approximately and temporarily, by furnishing immense amounts of new energy to the system, for sooner or later the law of entropy will overtake the system and destroy its dynamic equilibrium. A self-caused entity such as G will of course not be subject to entropy and thus cannot degenerate.

59. See for example William S. Hatcher, *The Logical Foundations of Mathematics,* Pergamon Press, Oxford, 1982.

60. Of course, in contrast to the boundary between categories one and two, the boundary between categories two and three is not objectively specifiable. Thus, we may not be able to determine, in a given instance, whether a certain principle is local or global. But our definition itself is objective (Platonistic) and does not depend on our being able to determine the boundary in all cases.

61. See H. A. Davidson, Avicenna's Proof of the Existence of God as a Necessarily Existent Being, *Islamic Philosophical Theology,* P. Morewedge, Editor, SUNY at Albany Press, Albany, 1979, pp. 165-187.

62. I owe to Professor Biryukov of the Moscow Institute for Foreign Relations this charming *reductio ad absurdum* of the use of modal logic in attempting to prove God's existence. The use of the same modality of necessity both to prove God, on one hand, and then to disprove Him, on the other, illustrates what Kant called the "antinomies of reason" in attempts to prove God. But the antinomial character of these arguments lies not in reason itself (i.e., in logic) but rather in the equivocal use of such terms as necessity and contingency.

63. For a detailed comparative discussion of the approach of these authors to the cosmological proof, see William Hatcher, *The Law of Love Enshrined,* op. cit.

64. See Bertrand Russell, *Why I am Not a Christian,* Allen and Unwin, London, 1958, pp. 145 ff.

65. For a more detailed discussion of this issue, see William Hatcher, *Logic and Logos,* op. cit., and *The Law of Love Enshrined,* op. cit.

66. Stephen Hawking, *A Brief History of Time,* Bantam Books, New York, 1988; expanded edition, 1998.

67. See William Hatcher, *Love, Power, and Justice: the Dynamics of Authentic Morality,* Bahá'í Publishing Trust, Wilmette, Ill., 1998, 2nd edition, 2002.

www.ingramcontent.com/pod-product-compliance
Lightning Source LLC
Chambersburg PA
CBHW031516040426
42445CB00009B/264